The Family Encounters
the Depression

ROBERT COOLEY ANGELL
Professor of Sociology, University of Michigan

ತ

GLOUCESTER, MASS.

PETER SMITH

1965

Copyright, 1936
By Charles Scribner's Sons

Reprinted, 1965
By Permission of Charles Scribner's Sons

TO

THE MEMORY OF

SARAH

A SISTER EVER CHEERFUL,
GENEROUS AND KIND

ACKNOWLEDGMENTS

During the course of this study I have had assistance of three kinds from friends and colleagues at the University of Michigan. I am happy to express my debt to Messrs. Richard Fuller, Henry Meyer and Frank Hartung for help in analyzing the data; to Dr. Theophile Raphael and Mr. Fuller for fruitful ideas with regard to the development of appropriate theory; and to Professors R. D. McKenzie and A. E. Wood for their reading of the manuscript and useful suggestions with respect to revision. As with all my efforts in sociology, the chief acknowledgment is due my uncle, the late Professor Charles Horton Cooley. For us, his students, there was enlightenment in his penetrating social theory and inspiration in his gentle dignity.

R. C. A.

CONTENTS

CHAPTER I

THE POINT OF DEPARTURE

THE present study had a dual purpose at its inception and has therefore a dual set of results. On the one hand, it has sought to find out something about the effect of the depression on family life, and, on the other, to make a contribution to the theory and method of social research. Since the former is the aspect which will have general interest, the body of this volume is devoted to an exposition of these substantive results and the theory derived from them. Considerations of sociological methodology are relegated to an appendix.

It hardly seems necessary to defend the appropriateness of a study of family life during a depression. Even though most observers agree that the family is playing a role of diminishing importance in the modern drama, no one can doubt its tremendous contemporary significance. The very fact that American sociologists have dealt with the family more than with any other institution shows that it still retains a central place in our culture. And what is more timely than an inquiry into the effect upon it of the great cataclysm we

I

call the depression? Surely the family has lain directly in the path of this rising tide and has therefore not escaped its onset. It is true that he who would secure sensational results had better investigate in other directions, for the family has great powers of resistance to sudden onslaughts. More rational and opportunist organizations like Chambers of Commerce and labor unions, on the one hand, and less vital ones like country clubs and lodges, on the other, would undoubtedly feel the effect of changed economic conditions more quickly and show them more obviously than the family. But the latter makes up in significance what it lacks in susceptibility. Though the effects we discover may be microscopic, they reveal shifts at a very basic level of social life.

In studying the adjustments which families make to a depression, we are coming about as near as social scientists ever get to the experimental method of their colleagues in the natural sciences. We have long envied the latter their ability to control all the significant conditions surrounding a particular process, so that they can vary first one factor and then another in order to determine the exact influence of each. What a beautiful example of the power of man's intellect to ferret out the secrets of his universe! How crucial may be the results for man's life! And how fortunate the investigator who has such remarkable techniques at his disposal! Though we in the social sciences

2

have our compensations, we have not, alas, well equipped laboratories whose searching gadgets can cut through the mazes of man's collective life to the very citadel of truth. We cannot arrange matters so as to allow only one factor to vary while holding all the rest constant.[1] No, not even if we are Soviet commissars. For the most part we must seek experiments which life, or God if you will, is already making. We must take advantage of chances like the present, where a sudden new force breaks in on a relatively stable complex of relations, for it is under such conditions that the effects of a particular cause can be grasped. The family, then, gives us our constants; the depression represents a marked change in one factor, income.

At the outset it is well to disabuse the reader's mind of any misconceptions regarding the scope of our inquiry. When one hears the term depression, one is likely to think of salary and wage cuts, unemployment, reduced budgets, foreclosed mortgages, crashing stock quotations and defaulted bonds. These seem, as indeed they are, the very signs and symbols of depression. When families encounter the depression, it is problems such as these with which they have to wrestle. Despite all this, these matters are of secondary

[1] I say this with full cognizance of the method of partial correlation which, it seems to me, can do this only very imperfectly because of the limited number of variables with which it can deal.

interest here. They are but incidents to our main concern, which, briefly, is to determine the effects of the depression upon the interrelationships among family members. This is a question in social psychology and social organization, not economics. And however much it may be necessary to learn about the economic situation, such knowledge is only preliminary to the discovery of what the depression has meant in terms of family relations.

In attacking a problem of this kind the investigator must first define it clearly in his own mind and then frame a method of research within the means at his disposal which will bring him as near as possible to fundamental analysis. The attempt to achieve a clear definition of the problem led to four limitations upon the families which were to be included in the study. First, permanent residence in the United States was required so as to ensure some homogeneity with reference to culture. Second, only "normal" families in the sense that parents and children were living together at the beginning of the depression were to be investigated. This eliminated homes broken by the death of one or both parents or by separation or divorce, and homes in which either there had been no children or they had grown up and moved away. To study such families too would have complicated the problem unnecessarily. Third, the families were further limited to those which had suffered a

4

severe decrease in income from accustomed sources—a decrease of at least 25 per cent in real income, to be exact. We cannot expect the results, therefore, to give any indication of the effect of the depression on all American families that are "normal" in the sense defined above. This is not to say that there have not been important influences on families whose income from accustomed sources decreased not at all or slightly, but only that it was felt necessary to confine this investigation to a more restricted problem. Fourth, it was stipulated that the decrease should have been "apparently lasting." This was to avoid the investigation of the effect of temporary unemployment, such as that due to seasonal lay-offs, for it was felt that our real concern was with family reactions to a more or less prolonged decrease.

From the delimitation of the problem let us now turn to the method of investigating it. A decision had to be made at the start as to whether to attempt a broad, statistical survey of a large number of families coming within the above limitations or an intimate case study of a much smaller number. The latter alternative was adopted because it was felt that the essence of the problem consisted in the effect of the decrease in income on internal family relations, an effect which could not be reached by the external indices available to the statistician. Matters of adjustment and integration are socio-psychological and require the use of

[handwritten margin note: takes example of a "normal" family—does not necessarily apply to all families]

5

sympathetic insight to bring them within the scientist's grasp.[1]

From the large number of American families made up of parents and children living together, which had suffered, since 1929, an apparently lasting decrease in real income of at least 25 per cent, a small number had to be selected for investigation. There are two radically different principles upon which this selection might have been based. The first employs the representative sample. This procedure would have required in our case that the investigator find out what proportion of all the above-described families were in certain classes with respect to income, number of members, national heritage, character of residence (rural or urban), length of marriage, and so on. Then he would have had to select his small sample so that it would contain corresponding proportions of families in these classes. By study of the families in the sample he would then have been able to discover what proportion of them possessed other characteristics, such as: more integration after the decrease, more dominance in one member of the family, etc. This would have shown trends, but would not have told us why cases, in many respects similar, showed some opposite characteristics. For example, one might have discovered that 75 per cent of the rural, white families, with incomes between $2000 and

---

[1] Attitude scales are an attempt to escape the dilemma here suggested. They were not used in this study. For a fuller discussion, see Appendix on Method.

6

$3000 became more integrated after the decrease, but one would then have been unable to determine why 25 per cent of them did not. This is the method of enumerative induction and is *not* the one used in this study.

The second method, that of analytic induction, does not attempt to secure a representative sample at all. Rather, it seeks to isolate distinctive types, each of which has its characteristic mode of adjustment, so that when one finds a family of a certain sort, one can predict how it will adjust to a severe decrease in income from accustomed sources. A good many families have to be studied in order to be sure to find at least one example each of the important types. If possible, it is desirable to have corroborative examples of each one in addition. This method, contrary to the first one, should throw light on causal relations. It is the one which I have attempted to carry out in this study.

Perhaps an analogy will make clearer the implications of analytic induction. Suppose we were interested in the effect of high wind on buildings. We might find by observation that some structures stand immobile, that some sway, that others bend or lean, and that others collapse. Furthermore, it might be possible to differentiate the original types which correspond with each of these results. Obviously this would not tell us how large a proportion of all buildings would fall down in a high wind, because we would not know what proportion of all buildings is of any particular type. Nor, if we investigated only a few buildings in our immediate vicinity, is it likely we would discover all the existing types. But our study might nevertheless be quite helpful in enabling us to forecast catastrophes and in increasing our knowledge of cause and effect in this field.

It may be noted that there is nothing to prevent the use of enumerative induction *after* the analytic induction has been accomplished. Once the types have been successfully analyzed one can count the frequency of their occurrence in any sample whatever in order to secure an idea of the relative importance of each type. This step, however, has not been taken in the present study.

In order to obtain complete documents concerning a number of families as a searching-ground for types, University of Michigan sociology students, whose own families (or, in a few instances, those of near relatives or close friends) met all the conditions, were persuaded to set down in great detail the activities, relations and attitudes characteristic of their families, both before and after the decrease.[1] Although a slightly larger number of documents was secured, only 50 were satisfactory

[1] Two requirements in addition to those enumerated above were established for the families to be analyzed. It was stipulated that no crucial event, unconnected with the depression, such as the death of one of the family members, should have occurred since the decrease; and also that the decrease should have come suddenly rather than over a long period. Both of these requirements were added so

enough to use. This would be a totally inadequate number for a representative sample, but, since our procedure is one of analytic rather than enumerative induction, the paucity of cases is not similarly damning here.

The validity of basing scientific conclusions upon evidence offered by one "participant observer" in each family without provisions for independent verification is, of course, highly questionable. A son or daughter is likely to be biased in various ways and may not give a truly "objective" account of matters. This was guarded against as far as possible by warning the writers in advance concerning the danger of subjectivity and checking over their analyses with them from this standpoint. Nevertheless corroboration would have been highly desirable, if it had been practicable.

We have, then, 50 American families whose lives we know both before and after a sudden and apparently lasting decrease of at least 25 per cent in real income from accustomed sources. What types can we find among them whose reactions to this situation seem specific?

as to secure families in which the effect of the decrease was uncomplicated and clearly evident.

The students were "persuaded" to write the documents by a remuneration made possible by a grant from the Faculty Research Fund of the University of Michigan.

9

CHAPTER II

FAMILY TYPES

BEFORE grappling with the problems of isolating types of American families, each of which will react characteristically to a decrease in income, we must obtain a precise notion of what the American family is from a general and inclusive point of view. What is the species of which the different types are but varieties?

Family life in this country today is the latest term of a long evolution, an evolution which has been influenced by many forces. Perhaps we can divide these forces into two sets—those which have made for strong family integration, and those which have tended to disorganize the family. In the former class we may put the heritage from the mediæval family with its inclusiveness of functions and its authoritative, patriarchal organization; the Puritan point of view in America with its emphasis on community control and a strict moral code; the isolation of families on the American frontier, requiring as it did family self-sufficiency and unity; and the fact that our democracy has been dominated by bourgeois property notions of family accumulation. On the other side of the ledger may be written the ideal of self-expression and personal freedom fostered by the Renaissance and the Reformation and gaining headway through the centuries; the emphasis of capitalism on individual initiative; the influence of the Industrial Revolution in removing industrial processes from the home; the development of modern communication which has generated ideals of democracy, and of personal opportunity and has thus encouraged extra-family associations; and the growth of city life where culture conflicts and confusion tend toward individualization.

The interplay of these forces has produced a paradoxical situation. We have, side by side, strong notions of family solidarity and the highest divorce rate of any modern nation; conventional sex mores and the emancipation of women; laws against the dissemination of birth control information and a rapidly falling birth rate. The American family has been in a state of rapid transition, which has often been called disorganization, for at least 50 years. Under these conditions we should expect wide variability and a minimum of common characteristics. Yet I think there is a solid core of beliefs and practices relative to family life which gives unity to the phrase, the American family, even today.

An enumeration of some of the ingredients which constitute this core may strengthen this contention. Monogamous wedlock is regarded as the normal channel for sex expression and the only proper

method of reproducing the species. The family is
the well-nigh universal way of rearing the young
and attempts are made to duplicate the family situation in those few cases where orphans have to be
cared for. The parents are charged with, and accept, the responsibility of providing for their children's welfare until they are grown. The children
in return are expected to help their parents when
they can and to respect their reasonable wishes.
Though children are no longer held completely
responsible for their parents' welfare in old age,
public sentiment strongly condemns children who
ignore the sufferings of their aged parents. The
father is looked upon as normally the chief breadwinner for the family, while the mother's principal
task is that of homemaker. And this is true even
though we must admit great differences in attitude
toward the wife's having a separate career. If she
does have a career it is usually considered subor-
dinate to that of her husband and to be enjoyed
only if her tasks as homemaker are not neglected.

These common characteristics are only a few
strands of the material which goes to make up each
American family. A great many other strands
vary in the highest degree so that each particular
web of family life shows some uniqueness of pattern. Our problem is to distinguish a few significant types among these innumerable patterns,
types which will show characteristic reactions to
decrease in income from accustomed sources. Any

generalizations which we make will of course only apply to contemporary American families. It is wholly within this compass that we are operating, and our types make no pretensions to universal validity.

We must first emphasize again that we are here concerned primarily with a socio-psychological entity—the family as a number of interacting personalities who are bound to each other by various sentiments and attitudes. This entity can be thought of as a structure of psychical interrelationships. From another point of view it appears to be an integration of personal roles or functions. The reader must bear constantly in mind that we are abstracting this socio-psychological whole from a life process where it is always commingled with the family as a sustenance or symbiotic unity. We are making a separation between two levels of interdependence, a separation somewhat artificial perhaps, but seemingly a necessary one as a scientific device. The terms which we use to describe family relations are therefore to be construed as applying only to the socio-psychological level, unless otherwise explicitly stated.

In dealing with the evolution of such a social form, an extremely useful concept is that of "the tentative process" as formulated by the late Professor Cooley.[1] According to this theory every structure grows by a selective process of trial and

[1] See *Social Process,* Chap. I.

error, developing in those directions which seem to "work" and inhibiting its activities in those directons which do not "take" in a social sense. Thus a constant process of adaptation to changing conditions goes forward.

Decrease in income is a condition which might well cause a family to enter on a new phase of this tentative process. Our question so far as types are concerned then becomes: What sorts of qualities are significant in determining how the family as a socio-psychological unit will react to the decrease? The answer which serious study of these 50 cases seems to give is: Integration and adaptability. It should be emphasized that the use of these criteria as the bases of our types was not a result of deductive reasoning from an *a priori* theory, but came out of much experimentation with conceptual schemes in actual analysis of the cases.[1] The criteria thus inductively arrived at do, however, harmonize with existing theory, since it is well recognized that external changes are accommodated to most easily where there is a maximum of integration and at the same time a maximum of flexibility.

We shall distinguish eight family types on this basis as follows:

Type I. Highly integrated, highly adaptable families.

   II. Highly integrated, moderately adaptable families.

[1] See Appendix on Method.

14

III. Highly integrated, unadaptable families.

IV. Moderately integrated, highly adaptable families.

V. Moderately integrated, moderately adaptable families.

VI. Moderately integrated, unadaptable families.

VII. Unintegrated, moderately adaptable families.

VIII. Unintegrated, unadaptable families.

These are obviously short-hand expressions which symbolize highly complex conditions that can only be grasped adequately through a thorough exposition of typical cases. But a few words of preliminary explanation may help to suggest the meaning of the terms.

Family integration, even when considering only the personal relations, is not a simple thing. There are many bonds of coherence and unity running through family life, of which common interests, affection, and a sense of economic interdependence are perhaps the most prominent.[1] In some instances, affection is strong but there is little community of interests or sense of economic interdependence; in others, the last is highly developed and the first only slightly. In fact almost every con-

[1] The sense of economic interdependence, a socio-psychological thing, is to be distinguished from economic interdependence itself, a symbiotic thing.

ceivable situation is encountered. Moreover, there is great variation in the interests which are common. Sometimes they are vocational, sometimes recreational, and sometimes there is one purpose, like the furnishing of the home, to which all adhere. Under these circumstances the only feasible procedure is to obtain an impression of solidarity in a general way by asking some such question as: "To what extent is this family making the most of its opportunities for the intra-family enrichment of the lives of its members?"

Adaptability is another complex consideration. We are concerned here, not with the adaptability of the family members as individuals, but with the adaptability of the unit in meeting obstacles in *its* way. It is possible for the individuals to be quite rational and open-minded in making their own private decisions, but for the family as a whole to be sluggish in adjusting to economic changes, because of a lack of any established habits of collective discussion and decision.

From reading these cases it seems that there are three principal conditions which may produce rigidity rather than flexibility in a family's structure. One is a materialistic philosophy of life among the members, or some of them, which makes them attach great significance to the standard of living to which they have been accustomed. Their material possessions and their sorts of recreation seem to them to fix the family's social status, so that a sharp decrease in expenditure would mean a loss of social role. They therefore are inclined to stay on the old level as long as possible and then to hide their fall from it by keeping up a good "front." This usually means a failure to adopt a rational budget, internal friction, and great unhappiness.

Another cause of rigidity is traditionalism in family mores. The husband who will not let his capable wife share in family control because he feels it is his role to be the sole leader is a case in point. Any belief or feeling, whether religious or moral or merely conventional, which hinders readjustment of member roles tends to produce incapacity to adapt to a crisis.

The third factor which the cases reveal is mere irresponsibility or happy-go-luckiness of one or both of the parents. When one of the principal family members is unable or unwilling to discipline himself in the interests of the whole there is necessarily a tardy if not a completely ineffectual readjustment. Not only is there no preparation for the rainy day, but even when the heavens open there is failure to seek shelter.

Thus the families which prove themselves most plastic and therefore, integration equal, best equipped to surmount obstacles, are the secularized, "modern" ones which do not put too great stock in material and pecuniary values and whose leading members are responsible and energetic. Families of this kind are perhaps most frequently found among thoroughly Americanized elements of the middle class, particularly in smaller cities. The metropolitan population seems to be more materialistic in its philosophy, while the farmers are likely to be traditional in outlook.

The reader will notice that there is no unintegrated, highly adaptable type. This was not intended, but is simply because there were no such families among our 50. We have no way of knowing whether or not further search would reveal families of such a type.

In order to give a clearer notion of the significance of the various terms, examples of five of the eight types are briefly outlined here. One must remember that these types refer to family structure before the decrease in income. Nothing will be said at this time concerning their encounter with, and readjustment to, the depression.

Type I. Highly Integrated, Highly Adaptable

CASE NO. 40[1]

There were four members of the Baxter family —father, mother, and a pair of twins, a boy and a girl. The parents were 44 and 43, the children 19. They lived in half of a 50-year-old double house in the better residential district of a Michigan town

---

[1] The cases throughout are identified by number. Other references to the same case can be found by consulting the Index of Cases on page 309.

known for its wealth and cultivated traditions. Their neighbors were a banker, a newspaper editor, a lawyer, two salesmen, a shoestore proprietor, the owner of a farm-implement store, a judge, and a carpenter. Less than three blocks away were the main street, the library, a grade school, three churches, a lumber yard, and a park. The house itself was one of the Victorian era, with high ceilings and a generous yard. Fine old elms shaded the yard and the street in front. Only the lower floor was wired for electricity and Welsbach burners were still used in the bedrooms.[1]

The furnishings of the house were in keeping with Mr. Baxter's income of $5000 a year and with his position in the community as an insurance agent and a county highway commissioner. There were several antique pieces of furniture and a tapestry or two. Other possessions included a radio, sporting equipment of various kinds, and an inexpensive automobile. The family also owned a cottage at a nearby lake and held a membership in a country club there.

Mr. Baxter was in good health, inclining a little toward stoutness, but energetic and interested in sports. He was cheerful and frank, a man who

[1] I have striven to make each illustrative case live for the reader by giving a rather complete picture. The facts are as given in the original documents, though summarized, with the exception of names, places and other identifying marks. I have protected the anonymity of the writers at all costs. Where direct quotations from the documents are given, I have sometimes taken the liberty to change tenses and to punctuate so as to make the meaning clear.

tried hard to win, but a good loser too. He neither took life lightly nor did he take it so seriously as to rob it of its joy. He read a good deal, considering how little time he had free from his two jobs. In magazines his taste ran to light fiction; and although many of the 100 or more books he read in a year were of the same sort, he occasionally perused a biography, an historical work, or a novel of the better type such as one of Galsworthy's. Though not a college man, his tastes were not dissimilar from those of the college men of the community.

His social and community activities were many. He was an officer in both the Chamber of Commerce and the Rotary Club and belonged to two lodges. He was very fond of bridge and was a member of two bridge clubs, one made up of married couples, the other a stag organization. His associates and friends were the leading citizens of the town. He was a vestryman of the Episcopal Church and faithful in attendance.

Mr. Baxter had not saved a great deal, partly because of the many calls on his pocketbook and partly because he was by nature generous. This was particularly true where the members of his own family were concerned, for he wanted them to have the best opportunities possible. He was a model husband and father and never showed any favoritisms or antagonisms within the family circle. Inclined to feel that his wife and his son were a little too idealistic in their conceptions, he charged this to lack of contact with the rude world of realities and was tolerant of their views.

Mrs. Baxter also was very energetic. In fact she tended to overdo. She was a member of the D. A. R., an officer of a woman's club and of the Board of Education, was in the guild of the Episcopal Church and active in the Michigan Federation of Women's Clubs. This was all in addition to her housework, which she did by herself, and very thoroughly. She had had a college education, specializing in music, and before her marriage had taught the piano. She did not read quite so much as her husband, for she found little time, but she took two women's magazines and a few club and political publications. Her other amusements were golf, bridge, and going to the movies.

It was due to her unceasing efforts that the home was so pleasant. She saw to it that the house and yard were kept in fine order, and she frequently rearranged rooms in order to vary the home and make it attractive. The Baxter household had a reputation for hospitality for which she should receive the chief credit.

Her position on the Board of Education brought a small salary which she saved, as far as possible, for the education of the children.

Her friends, like her husband's, were drawn from the most highly educated circles in the community and she was considered more or less of a leader among them. Her attitude toward the rest of the family was one of sincere affection and helpfulness. She shared both triumphs and disappointments. Her one weakness was an extreme sensitivity to what others said, especially family members, so that she was frequently hurt by trivial remarks which really had no significance.

Marjorie was a slight girl of medium height, whose healthy freshness and pretty features made her extremely attractive. She had, however, suffered at one time from infantile paralysis, and, though this had left no external mark, she was not as strong as she appeared to be. She had learned to swim, dance, and otherwise enjoy the recreations of her friends. Her nature was a sunny, cheerful one and she was known for her "pep."

At this time she was in a small college, a happy member of a sorority and doing excellently in her studies. Her particular interests were music and dramatics. She loved to read, principally novels and plays. Her best friend was winning state honors in public speaking and debating.

She too made family life pleasant for the rest. She was frank, sincere and thoughtful. Though capable of penetrating observation and criticism, she never offered her opinions in a malicious spirit. Like her mother she was somewhat sensitive of others' criticism of her.

Harlow* was larger than his sister, very tall

---

* The writer of the case history is designated in each instance by an asterisk.

and rather slim. Like the rest he was energetic, but perhaps a little more nervous than the others. He had engaged all through high school in many branches of sports and had kept himself in constant training.

His personality was an odd mixture of sincerity and cynicism. He was loyal and devoted to his family and friends but was at the same time somewhat contemptuous of the "great unwashed" public. He was serious and conscientious to a fault. Reading took a great deal of his time. Beside the usually youthful taste for fiction and adventure stories, he had a real fondness for substantial works dealing with economic and political problems. He was the type to enjoy chess and studious bridge, as well as outdoor sports.

He was at this time attending the same college as his twin sister. There he was a fraternity member, class officer, advertising manager of the college paper and a member of the tennis and basketball teams. His only earnings were $2.50 a week from his newspaper work. His friends were the active and more intelligent students on the campus.

Though a little thoughtless at times around the house, he was a son of whom his family could be proud and he, in his turn, appreciated the other members and how much they were doing for him.

The Baxters are interesting from an historical viewpoint. Mrs. Baxter's lineage was distinguished, and there were artists, judges, writers, and editors among her living relatives. The family, however, took on no airs and had worked hard to earn itself a position in the community, especially since the time of a bankruptcy just after the War. That they had succeeded in this endeavor is attested by the high opinion in which they were held by the people of the community.

The social organization of the family was a closely woven texture with the mother at the center. She, more than any one else, had a definite ideal and definite plans for reaching it. It was she to whom all turned for consultation and advice. Mrs. Baxter and Marjorie were closer to one another than any other pair, but there was no exclusiveness in their relation. The twins were conscious of the pride their parents had in them and the ambitions for their future, so that it was their chief care not to disappoint these high expectations.

Family life was not always harmonious, but the little frictions were such as soon to disappear in the wider stream of family interests and hopes. Temporary annoyance was often due to the frank criticism given, but in the long run this was not a disrupting but an integrating factor, for it emphasized the interdependence of the members.

The Baxters did a good deal together. They frequently played golf, or bridge, went driving, or attended church or a movie as a group. Every Sunday night they held open house and their friends dropped in to pop corn, play simple games, **and** otherwise enjoy a sociable evening.

The "we" feeling in this family was very strong. One never thought of his own welfare alone. Though the objectives of the family were never consciously enunciated and discussed, there was a felt unity of purpose which was very powerful.

The principal type features are plainly shown in this case. Integration is strongly in evidence. High adaptability is perhaps not positively demonstrated, but there is no indication of anything which would get in the way of quick and rational adaptation to a decrease in income. The fact that the family had fought its way up from one bankruptcy is certainly some evidence of its ability to meet adversity.

Type IV. *Moderately Integrated, Highly Adaptable*

CASE NO. 51

The Standishes lived in a large old-fashioned house in the midst of a Michigan village. At the time of the decrease, Mr. Standish was 56, his wife was 47, the two girls were 21 and 17, and the boy 19. Since Mr Standish had been a mining engineer and at this time was a lumberman with an income of about $4000, the family was regarded as one of the more substantial ones in the community.

Mr. Standish was a large, strong man, weighing 190. The only illness that he had suffered for a long time was sinus trouble. He was tremendously energetic, frequently arising at four or five o'clock in the morning and working tirelessly until supper time. His self-confidence was enormous, but at the same time he was very friendly, and was generous to those in need. Once he had bought a through ticket for an old man whom he picked up on the road who was trying to get to relatives in California.

Mr. Standish's chief weakness was his impetuosity. He rushed into things without sufficient investigation and often had occasion to regret it. He had always put back whatever he saved into real estate, so that the family had large holdings, but nothing laid by in the bank or in liquid investments. He paid his men high wages and was known as an honest, capable business man.

Since Mr. Standish had done a good deal of prospecting in his younger days, had been a semi-professional ball player, and had knocked around lumber camps, he had a number of crudities of manner and speech which made some of the more cultured neighbors regard him as "low-brow." But his wife had smoothed many of the rough edges and his varied experiences made him an interesting conversationalist. He was not attracted by the more

26

formal kinds of social activity, preferring the family circle or a few close friends. Though a member of two lodges, he was a poor member, and he took no active part in athletic teams or clubs. Travel had always been his principal hobby, but recently he had bought a farm and had taken great interest in its operation.

At home, he was usually cheerful and never complained about family expenses. He was a kind husband and father, though he occasionally became angry without much provocation and would have dominated his wife if she had let him. Perhaps his most unseemly trait in personal intercourse was his tendency to ridicule others in what seemed to be a mean way.

Mrs. Standish had not been in good health for several years. She had undergone several operations which had left her nervous and desirous of doing more than her strength would allow. Rather an emotional woman, she was at the same time kindly and moody. Her Christian faith meant much to her, but she took no active part in church affairs. She could be very entertaining when feeling well. One of the sources of disagreement between her husband and herself was her desire to go out to shows. However, she shared with him a dislike for card parties and other organized forms of sociability. Her membership in the Eastern Star meant no more to her than did his in the Masons to him. Her main recreation was working around the house and yard, for she delighted in making them more attractive.

Mrs. Standish was more cautious than her husband and equally sincere. She was an affectionate mother and her interest in her children led her to back the Girl Scout movement in the community. Her friends were the leading women of the village, and though she was kind to all, she was particular whom she admitted to her friendship.

Within the family, she felt closest to the two younger children. Mr. Standish's family had, at an earlier time, been unkind to her, and she felt that he and the elder girl resembled in some respects these relatives to whom she was hostile.

Dorothy, the older girl, was a steady worker, but inclined to be moody. When she was melancholy she was disagreeable to the rest of the family. She, like her mother, was a devout Christian and her moral standards were very high. Like her father, she was fond of conversation. She had a mind of her own, knew what she wanted, and went straight for it. Consequently she was not one to be "bossed" with impunity. No one doubted her sincerity or her ability. At this time she was a high ranking college student. She had friends of both sexes but she did not go out for college activities or sports. She enjoyed sewing and reading and led a quiet life, being especially careful in expenditures. Her disagreeable streak was especially prominent in her relations with her sister, of whom she was jealous.

28

Walter,* though possessing a good physique, was not particularly energetic and took things rather easily. He was a conscientious, sincere, moral, and fairly bright young man who was more interested in travel books than in sports. That he was popular with his associates is shown by the fact that he had been elected a class officer several times during his school career. He had worked at odd jobs from time to time and was of a saving nature. His close friends were few and he was fond of being by himself. His home meant a great deal to him and he was particularly attached to his mother. Though he quarrelled sometimes with his sisters, he would stand up for them too when the occasion demanded.

Lillian was more of an extrovert than either of the others. She was always "in things," liked to spend her money, was very popular, and had a frank, attractive personality. She had an even temperament and showed less jealousy or favoritism than any other member of the family.

The position of the Standish family in the community was this: The wealthier and more highly educated families mingled with them with a certain condescension because of Mr. Standish's crudeness; but Mrs. Standish and the children regarded the family as an intellectual one and therefore felt that they were superior to most of the families in the town.

Because of Mrs. Standish's bad health, Mr.

29

Standish, Walter, and Lillian had become accustomed to letting her have her way around the house. Dorothy, however, often refused to be led by her mother. If a real issue developed, Mr. Standish was likely to side with Dorothy against the other three. However, these troubles were the exception, and usually family life went along smoothly. The members did many things together, the children helped around the house and yard to some extent (though Lillian in particular was likely to be somewhere else when she was wanted) and there was a strong sense of a hospitable home to which friends were always welcome. Discipline was sympathetic, but the children knew that they were expected to live up to high standards.

Mr. and Mrs. Standish had always taken an interest in their children's education and had given them encouragement and help. Good magazines were taken and an opportunity was given each child to develop along musical lines.

It is obvious why this family is classified as moderately integrated rather than highly integrated, for there were real, though perhaps not serious, lines of cleavage. The father's indifference to his crudities was galling to the others and the friction between Dorothy and her mother was more than a passing thing. On the other hand, there is no evidence of lack of adaptability and we therefore rate the family highly in that respect.

Type V. Moderately Integrated, Moderately Adaptable

CASE NO. 3

There were three generations in the Haskins household—the maternal grandmother, aged 75, the parents, both 49, and three children, boys of 20 and 17, and a girl of 15. They lived in a fashionable suburb of Detroit where they were surrounded by well-to-do neighbors whose houses cost from $20,000 to $30,000. Their house was of moderate size, well furnished, and equipped with electric refrigerator, electric range, and other modern devices. The family income of about $16,000 enabled them to keep a Packard car, to have a maid who came in by the day, and in addition a laundress and scrubwoman who came two days a week.

Mr. Haskins was in the real-estate and insurance business. He had risen to the presidency of a brokerage which was a very successful firm. He was a steady worker, not nervous, rarely angry. His health had always been excellent and he possessed a fine physique—6 feet 2 inches tall and weighed 170. He had been a physical instructor in the army during the War.

His sense of humor was notable and he was constantly joking at dinner table. This trait led to his keen enjoyment of Robert Benchley, Donald

Ogden Stewart, and other writers of this sort. His reading was not confined to this type of book, however, for he read much serious literature. His other forms of recreation were golf, touring, fishing and hunting in Canada, and, above all, bridge. He was an expert at the latter game and enjoyed some prestige in the neighborhood on that basis. His friends were business men of his own type who were members of his clubs.

Though he liked to spend money on cars and on vacation trips to Canada or Florida, he was cautious in money matters and never played the stock market. He paid all bills promptly and wished the other members of the family to be methodical with the allowances which he gave them.

He was a trifle reserved, even within the family circle. Though always just in dealing with the children, he was usually firm. The only exception had been his leniency toward the younger boy, William, who had been expelled from school for misdemeanors.

Mrs. Haskins had not been very well for some time. She had had several operations. Her desire to entertain and go out socially made her do too much and left her nervous and irritable. She was vivacious outside the family circle, but within it was inclined to be short-tempered and cross. Occasionally, however, she was very amusing. Her "society" interests led to an emphasis on etiquette, which sometimes annoyed the children. She was fond of playing bridge and also enjoyed going with her husband on trips. Her friends were of the "bridge club" type.

Mrs. Haskins had complete control of the household budget, but was not particularly economical or efficient in this capacity. She bought new furnishings more often than seemed necessary to the rest, and spent excessive amounts entertaining. To the children she was generous, but favored first one and then another, thus causing jealousies.

Her angry outbursts toward other members of the family were discounted as resulting from her poor health. She never quarrelled with her husband, but found it very difficult to get along with her mother, who held notions about raising the children which Mrs. Haskins considered old-fashioned.

Mrs. Williams, the grandmother, was in fair health for her age. She also tried to do more than her health made wise. Her recreations were reading and automobile riding. She tried to aid with the housework, but her efforts hindered rather than helped. She was very economical, and spent her $40 a month pension from the government frugally. (Her husband had been a captain in the Civil War). Her one extravagance was gifts to the children. She played no favorites in this, but she was more fond of Franklin, the older boy, than of the rest, probably because she had taken care of him for some time when he was a baby.

Franklin* was a tall, healthy university student, bright, but rather superficial in his academic work. He carefully avoided introspection and was inclined to live a pleasurable sort of existence. He worked in the summer time and bought his clothes out of his earnings. Like his father, he was punctual in payment of bills. His principal recreations were horseback riding, canoeing, tennis, shooting, bridge, and reading. His friends were fraternity men and sorority girls of good character. In the family, he felt sorry for his grandmother and tried to make things pleasant for her. He was critical of his younger brother for his high-school misbehavior and his general thoughtlessness. For his father he had the highest respect.

William was a lad of a good deal of capacity, but lazy and easy-going. Bland and self-assured, he was a brilliant writer for his age and had worked spasmodically for the high-school paper. He had never worked during vacations and even neglected his chores around the house. Golf, cards, and reading were his amusements, and he mingled with a questionable set of youngsters of an irresponsible type. He was constantly borrowing money from other members of the family and had no notion of saving. He had even resorted to poker playing and selling old clothes to raise funds. He was not at all companionable with the rest of the family. He

34

disregarded his parents' wishes frequently and would not associate with his brother.

Marie was in junior high school at this time. She was more like Franklin than like William. A good student, but a little lazy, she was energetic in her play and enjoyed swimming and horseback riding. She was beginning to go out with boys and liked to buy clothes. However, she was in general frugal and saved her allowance. She idolized her father and mother, was somewhat resentful toward her grandmother who constantly criticized her notions, and sided with Franklin against William, who teased her.

The Haskins were very proud of their lineage, which extended back beyond the Revolution in this country to aristocratic English ancestors. On the living-room wall was the family coat of arms. William was the only one who did not take his lineage seriously.

The household seemed to be organized on a rather individualistic basis. Whatever leadership there was was exercised by Mr. Haskins. There were some family "affairs" such as Sunday afternoon rides with the grandmother, but the children usually participated half-heartedly and unwillingly. During Christmas and birthday celebrations there was a more genuine sense of solidarity. There was very little sharing of troubles or ambitions. Each one kept his affairs very much to himself. Thus, although there was considerable family pride in

35

an abstract sort of way, there was a minimum of co-operative activity and experience.

———

We see here a family which falls <u>short of true</u> <u>integration</u> on several counts, but which, on the other hand, is still <u>far from unintegrated</u>. With regard to <u>adaptability</u> it seems also to fall into an <u>intermediate</u> category. The obvious delight which Mrs. Haskins and William took in the things which money can buy, to say nothing of the real, though less marked, inclination toward a pecuniary set of values of the others, indicates a tendency toward rigidity, though not an extreme one. One feels that Mr. Haskins has the family well enough in hand so that <u>reasonable adjust-</u> <u>ments could be made</u>. Hence, the family qualifies as <u>moderately adaptable</u> rather than unadaptable.

Type VI. Moderately Integrated, Unadaptable

CASE NO. 5

The Underwood family was composed of the two parents, the maternal grandmother and a boy of 20. They lived in an apartment in one of the more exclusive sections of New York City, for which they paid $250 a month. Mr. Underwood was the owner of a small manufacturing business with an income of about $10,000 a year. They owned a Pierce Arrow car and were inclined to

36

take a condescending air toward other people in
the same apartment building whom they felt were
not of such "good families" as they. There was
considerable pride in their English ancestry.

Mr. Underwood was a healthy, hard-working,
cheerful sort who did not trust his subordinates
to do things right and so took an unnecessary load
of detail on his own shoulders. He was known as
an honest, capable business man. His wants were
few and he did not spend much; his only extravagances were a well-stocked liquor cabinet and a
taste for drama and opera. What things he did
want, he wanted to be of the best quality.

His friends were hearty, bluff men, good company, and not boisterous. Due to a leg injury in
youth he could play no games except golf, and he
only indulged in this sport occasionally. To the
members of his family he was kind, affectionate
and self-sacrificing. His home was his principal
interest.

Mrs. Underwood had been a very beautiful
younger woman and was still handsome. She was
very energetic, but very nervous too, a great wor-
rier, particularly where her only child was concerned. Her friends were chiefly interested in
bridge, women's clubs, and social work. She spent
a good deal in entertainment, frequently drawing
on her husband when she had exhausted her own
bank account. She did not care much for reading
and had no outdoor recreations. The church

seemed to mean much to her and she was regular in attendance. Her relations with other members of the family were harmonious but hardly close.

The grandmother was "a distinguished looking old English lady, cheerful, unworldly, wrapped up in her grandson, and a source of joy to her daughter, because of her ability to carry on an intelligent conversation. She may be summed up by the statement that she was still living in the '90's."

Robert,* the only child, was a freshman at college at this time. He had always been healthy, and interested in sports, but when he got away from home he revelled in his freedom and began to do all the things he had been warned not to do—gambling, drinking, etc.—which put him in bad condition and ruined his chances for success in athletics. His attitude toward life was cynical and mocking. He had a very materialistic set of values and had few real friends because "of his tendency to take all and give nothing." He was extravagant, had never saved, and showed little gratitude for what his family did for him. His attitude of condescension extended even to his own parents, whom he regarded as a little old-fashioned. He criticized them freely and thought his judgment superior to theirs.

Almost the only common activity participated in by the Underwoods was church attendance on Sundays and on Christmas. Otherwise each went his own way. There was family pride and con-

38

siderable affection, but an individualistic spirit and lack of co-operation. Mr. Underwood kept to his sphere, the earning of the family living, and he left his wife to manage domestic affairs. Robert had been given all the opportunities in the way of education that money could buy, but he showed little appreciation of them.

––––––

The propriety of cataloging the Underwoods as a moderately rather than a highly integrated family is hardly open to question. They certainly achieve nothing like an ideal unity. The reasons for regarding them as unadaptable may not be quite so apparent. A careful reading of the case, however, gives one the feeling that the mother and son particularly, and the father and grandmother in lesser degree, are very strongly attached to their material comforts and the standard of living which they have had. In addition, there is irresponsibility in at least two members, which leads one to suspect that they would not trim their sails until they absolutely were forced to. Unadaptable therefore seems a proper characterization.

Type VI. Unintegrated, Moderately Adaptable

CASE NO. 46

The Clarks lived in Pontiac, Michigan, where Mr. Clark had been for many years a foreman over the watchmen and elevator men in an automobile factory. He was 48, his wife was 44, there was a married daughter living in the same city, a boy in college who did not return even in the summer, except for a brief visit, and a little girl, aged nine. Thus there were really only three in the household group at this time. Their six-room house was one of a large number that the automobile company had built and sold to its employees. The families in the neighborhood were those of better-paid workers, and their yards and houses were well kept up. The Clarks' furniture was adequate and kept in good condition. They owned an inexpensive car, and they were in the habit of getting a new one every two years. Mrs. Clark had a fur coat, Mr. Clark belonged to a lodge, the home contained a radio and a telephone, and they entertained occasionally, all of which showed a high standard of living for a worker's family.

Mr. Clark was short and stocky, a little inclined to stoutness. He was very strong, both because of constant work and because of an emphasis throughout his life on physical recreation. He had had some college training and was fond of reading, but his eyes were rapidly giving out. Though a very sincere person, he was inclined to be dogmatic, and was very short-tempered when crossed. He had a few friends but indulged little in social activities. However, he belonged to a patriotic organization. He was distant, even to the members of his own family. Quiet and detached, he never seemed to "warm up" to any one. He had no ideal of a united, co-operative family life. He seemed to be quite willing that the members of the family should live together under one roof without any close ties of affection. The two older children had had to earn all their own money from an early age. Because of this lack of any feeling that he should help them get started in the world, these children had become bitter toward their father.

His wife had a mild, easy-going, compromising temperament, but she was somewhat weary of the drudgery of continuous hard work. She none the less managed to maintain a certain optimism. Her principal job was the running of the household. Her hobbies were music and raising flowers. She, like her husband, belonged to a patriotic society. Her relatives and the neighbors with whom she was friendly were very fond of her. Her usual cheerfulness made her a pleasant companion. She was quite close to her children, but seemed to have little depth of affection for her husband.

Arthur,* the boy away at college, was hard-working, serious and intelligent. He had supported himself entirely since leaving high school. His sense of the unfairness of his father's treatment of himself and his older sister had led him to stay away from home except for Christmas and occasional week-ends.

Alice, the nine-year-old daughter, had been indulged much more than either of the other children, and was consequently a little spoiled.

Although Mr. and Mrs. Clark cherished a secret ambition to have their children succeed, both intellectually and economically, Mr. Clark's theory seemed to be that this would come to pass only if they were left to fight their own battles. The married daughter and Arthur, brought up in this way, had very little "home" feeling. Despite this, they felt affection for their parents.

The family had always been dominated by the father. His word was law, and no project of which he disapproved received any backing from him. The answer of the children had been revolt. Mrs. Clark had tried to be the go-between and diplomat of the family, but with slight success. Solidarity was almost entirely of the bread-and-butter or symbiotic variety. There were no common activities except the meals. Christmas and Thanksgiving celebrations were the only family occasions.

———

In this instance there seems to be no doubt of the validity of a low rating in integration. One child at least has left home because of antagonism to his father's ideas. The placing of the family in this type rather than Type VIII, however, is not so clearly justifiable. The father's inclinations toward dogmatism might lead one to regard this

as an unadaptable family. On the side of plasticity
are to be reckoned, however, the carefulness with
which the family has always watched its budget,
the lack of any notion that the father is to be the
sole breadwinner, and the self-sufficiency of the
various members.

―――――

These five illustrative cases serve to indicate the
character of the type system here adopted and the
reader can, without much difficulty, imagine the
sort of family which falls into each of the three
types not exemplified. In any event each type will
receive extended treatment in the chapters to
follow.

CHAPTER III

THE PRESSURE OF THE DECREASE IN INCOME

A DECREASE in income from accustomed sources is an economic or pecuniary fact, not a sociological one. Since we are concerned with the socio-psychological structure of family relations we must translate such a decrease into terms which represent its ⌐sociological stimulus⌐ value.⌐ When one attempts to do this, one soon discovers that he has to deal, not with one degree of pressure but with several, irrespective of the type of family being considered. Upon the same type of family we must assume that similar forces have similar effects, but a decrease in income is not always the same force. Nor is it a question of the amount of the decrease. A 25-per-cent one may have much the same effect as a 75-per-cent one.[1] It is rather a question of the amount of pressure on the socio-psychological structure of interrelationships. A decrease alone represents some pressure, but there is much more if the decrease entails in addition a shift in the positions of family members on the

[1] See Appendix on Method for proof of this statement.

44

symbiotic or sustenance level. Thus if the decrease means that a son becomes the chief wage earner in place of the father, the pressure is greater than if there has been a mere decrease in the sole bread-winner's income, even though the decrease is larger in the latter case than in the former.

It may seem strange to many to treat a shift in the symbiotic positions of family members as an integral part of the pressure to which the family must adjust, for this is already an adaptation. But it is an adaptation on a different level, a level below the socio-psychological one with which we are concerned. These changes in position are so much a matter of immediate expediency that the family type as defined in the last chapter makes little difference. What has to be done for bread and butter purposes will usually be done. The decrease with its accompanying position changes, then, becomes the pressure to which the structure of personal interrelations, defined by attitudes and sentiments, has to adjust. It is in meeting similar problems of this kind that our different types of family react differently.

Throughout this study we will use the terms "member position" and "member role." The former refers to the symbiotic level, the latter to the socio-psychological level. A change in positions requires, if integration is to be maintained, a corresponding adjustment of roles. A flexible family can achieve this. But if the change in positions

45

is not followed by a redefinition of the functions of family members, in other words a readjustment of their roles, then the integration is almost certain to suffer. Thus, if a wife becomes the chief bread-winner in place of her husband, and the family is not plastic enough to rationalize this adequately in a new set of concepts of member roles, the decrease will prove disastrous.

We shall distinguish three degrees of severity in the impinging force of the decrease:—A decrease entailing similar positions, one entailing modified positions, and one entailing changed positions. Since the parents' positions are more firmly established than the children's and shifts in them are more upsetting, it is these chiefly which we have to consider in determining the severity of the decrease as a sociological force. If a son starts to work at a small wage but the father remains the chief support of the family, the decrease is termed one with similar positions, because there is no seriously disturbing change in symbiotic function.

This term, "similar positions," is used to cover a whole range of practical situations, from that one in which the positions remain identical, through situations of minor shift, until the limiting case is reached, beyond which the next term, "modified positions," is used. In order to indicate the extent of the range, a case near this borderline is given here. The reader may assume that all less serious deviations would be classed as "similar positions."

46

Decrease with Similar Positions

CASE NO. 21

Case No. 21, that of the Harrison family, shows them originally as a family of five living in a small Indiana town. Mr. Harrison was the secretary and treasurer of a farm-implement company and was the sole support of the family, with an income of $6000. His older daughter was in a nurse's training school and helped him in the office in the summer time. The boy was in a local engineering college, and the younger daughter in high school.

The decrease came as a result of the bankruptcy of Mr. Harrison's firm. He secured another position at $1200 very quickly and managed to buy a gas station for his son from his savings. The latter is now operating this station and contributing most of its $600 income to the family. The older daughter has graduated from the nursing school and makes just about as much as her father. She also turns most of this in to the family. The positions of the mother and younger daughter have not changed.

The fact that the father's position as the economic backbone has not been changed makes it seem proper to characterize this as a "similar positions" case even though he no longer makes the bulk of the family income. Because the boy is

47

careless and the daughter is away from home a great deal, neither of them has displaced Mr. Harrison at all. Indeed, the girl is doing what it was expected she would do, anyway. All in all, we cannot say that the slight shift here makes the decrease much more of an obstacle to family readjustment than it would have been if positions had remained exactly the same.

———

As a contrast to No. 21 we might examine No. 11 which seems to be a typical instance of "modified positions."

Decrease with Modified Positions

CASE NO. 11

The Daley household just before the decrease was made up of mother, father, and daughter, 18. There were two married sons. At this time Mr. Daley held a skilled factory job and was the sole breadwinner for the family. His wife was in complete charge of the household and its budget. Mary was attending a local junior college.

The decrease came as a result of the growing irregularity of Mr. Daley's employment, which was in an automobile factory. His yearly income fell to less than a third of what it had been—from $2000 to $600. This necessitated Mary's leaving college and finding a job. In this she succeeded, and her job in a bank is now a more certain source of income than her father's employment. She works every day, whereas he is lucky to work two days a week. Because Mr. Daley is home so much and helps his wife with the housework, his family position has been modified, and Mary is looked to more and more as the mainstay of the family in the outside world.

———

This situation is a more radical shift than that exemplified by Case No. 21, but is considerably less radical than the one termed "changed positions." We will now turn to a case in which this concept finds exemplification, Case No. 36.

Decrease with Changed Positions

CASE NO. 36

The Yorks were a family of three, father, mother, and boy, 21. Mr. York had turned from the field of research chemistry to real estate at the age of 45 because he wanted to make a better living. He had been successful in his new career and, just prior to the decrease, was making an income of $10,000. Mrs. York was mainly interested in her home, though bridge clubs were her favorite recreation. Charles was a university student, dependent upon his father.

The depression caused Mr. York's business to fail, and his income dropped to nothing. He found nothing else to do. Mrs. York saved the day by turning her unusual ability at bridge to account. She became a teacher and soon worked up a large and fairly lucrative clientele. Her income is now about $2500 a year. Thus the husband and wife positions are almost completely reversed, because he now looks after many of the household duties while she is away teaching. The son is economizing as much as possible, but is still pursuing his college career, and is not contributing to the family income.

The York family is so perfect an illustration of what is meant by changed positions that no further comment on this concept seems necessary.

Now that we have distinguished certain original family types and have differentiated three degrees of severity in the impinging pressure, we are in a position to discuss the theoretical relationship between the two. Obviously when a particular type of family is subjected to a particular sort of pressure the result must always be the same if the process is to be encompassed by scientific generalizations. What conceptual tools have we for dealing with these results?

Where there is a well-defined social structure, an external pressure must, it seems to me, bring

about one of three conditions: (1) no change, because the particular structure is able to resist the
pressure without internal reorganization; (2) a
maintenence of structure, though a modified one,
because facile readjustment takes place to meet the
pressure; or (3) an impairment or disintegration
of structure, because the existing organization is
neither able to cope with the pressure nor to shift
so as to do so.[1] If the last result ensues we may
say that the type is vulnerable to the particular
pressure involved; if either the first or second, that
it is invulnerable. To differentiate the first result
from the second we may call the former firm invulnerability and the latter readjustive invulnerability.

We should expect to find families firmly invulnerable either when they have had to resist similar
pressure in the past, or when they have foreseen
the possibility of such pressure and prepared for
it, or finally, when their structure is such as to
withstand the pressure even though not foreseen.
Readjustive invulnerability is particularly likely to
occur, if at all, in connection with a decrease involving modified or changed positions. These
shifts on the symbiotic level usually require corresponding shifts on the socio-psychological one, so
that a new pattern of roles is established. If the
family proves itself capable of this fluid equilibrium we are still warranted in judging it invul-

[1] Compare Florian Znzniecki, *The Method of Sociology,* pp. 12–
16, 297–8.

51

nerable to the particular pressure involved. Family structures which prove vulnerable do so usually both because they lack adaptability and because the impinging pressure is unexpected and strange.

All that has just been said applies only to families which are originally integrated. The two unintegrated types, VII and VIII, appear to defy analysis in terms of vulnerability and invulnerability. The reason seems to be that these families do not have sufficient structure in the first place to resist pressure. Any impinging force will change a loosely knit, individualistic family, and, as the pressure increases, the changes become greater. It is as if one were dealing with a jellyfish. The harder you poke it, the more it will yield at points of attack, but there can hardly be said to be a breaking of its structure.

These varying results of course are not permanent. They are stages in a process, the tentative process of social development. What we are actually doing is taking a short period in the evolution of various families, a period marked in each case by a severe decrease in income, and observing what happens in the brief time that we have them under the microscope. Where a family manages to remain firmly invulnerable to the pressure of the decrease, there is no internal adjustment at all. In the other two cases, the tentative process is going forward in different ways. A situation of readjustive invulnerability is one in which the family has such potentialities for meeting change that the process of adjustment is immediate and satisfactory, with the result that the family structure remains intact, though altered. It is like radically remodelling the inside of one's house while still continuing to live comfortably in it. On the other hand, a situation of vulnerability means that the family organism, if we may use that term, is definitely wounded and thus weakened.

The distinctions between these differing results are not clean cut. There is bound to be a little readjustment in every case and it therefore becomes a question of degree as to where to draw the line between firm and readjustive invulnerability. Similarly, there are families which show a short period of disorganization at the first shock and then readjust, so that they recover their integration quickly. Are these to be classed as vulnerable or as readjustively invulnerable?

Such questions lead to the realization that, given more time, many, perhaps most, families which prove vulnerable would regain their integration. In other words they are going through a painful process which involves disorganization and reorganization instead of the painless process represented by the term "readjustive invulnerability." Since this study includes such a short time span we see only the disorganization phase in these cases.

Another factor which complicates our problem is that a family is a structure which inevitably experiences internal growth. This is especially true of the families we are concerned with because the method of selection was such as practically to insure the presence of children of college age. These children would probably have been taking on new responsibilities irrespective of the depression, so that the pattern of family life would have been changing to some extent anyway. One must regard such readjustment as normal and not to be confused with the readjustment taking place as a response to the decrease. It is easier to state this, however, than it is actually to disentangle the two streams of tentative process which are involved.

The scheme of analysis which has been outlined represents, as must all scientific procedures, a radical abstraction from real life. Try as we will to find families which are proceeding "normally" except for the impact of the depression, there must be many varying factors in each case which destroy its complete typicality. Such variations cannot be excluded from the cases nor can they be included in the conceptual set-up. They are the fortuitous elements or events which we have to allow for in arriving at generalizations, but which are ignored in the generalizations themselves.

CHAPTER IV

HIGHLY INTEGRATED, HIGHLY ADAPTABLE FAMILIES

THIS is the first of eight chapters, each of which is devoted to the consideration of one of our family types. For each type the effect of the less severe pressures will be discussed before the effect of the more severe ones. All three pressure situations are not represented among the cases found in every type, so that the picture will sometimes be incomplete. We can, however, interpolate or extrapolate tentatively and thus sketch in the missing portions. In order to make the presentation less abstract, cases will be used as illustrations of the various sequences of type-pressure-effect.

There were 12 Type I families in our series, families which originally showed both high integration and high adaptability. Of these, 8 suffered a decrease with similar positions; 3 a decrease with modified positions; and 1 a decrease with changed positions. As an illustration of the first group we may take Case No. 32.

CASE NO. 32

The Browns are a family of four. When the decrease began to be felt in 1931 the father was

49, the mother 42, and the two girls, 21 and 19. They lived in the lower flat of a two-family brick dwelling, which they owned, in a fairly good residential section of Chicago. The home was well furnished and the family possessed a piano, a radio, a Ford roadster and a Chrysler sedan. The upper flat was rented for $65 a month, and a bungalow, which the family also owned, brought another $50. A lot on which the family hoped to build, had been purchased for $6000, in an exclusive residential suburb.

Mr. and Mrs. Brown had both been born in Ontario, but had lived in Chicago since their marriage. He had started out as a barber, had later organized a barber college, and finally branched into the medical-supply business. This venture had succeeded and the business was bringing him about $5000 a year. Like many others, he was trying to make some money on stocks, but he bought them outright, not on margin. However, the Browns had not denied themselves present pleasures, for they had a summer-resort cottage, a family membership in a golf club at the resort, and had taken, in 1928, an auto trip to California. Both the girls were being sent to a small college.

Mr. Brown was industrious, careful and optimistic. He decided all pecuniary matters and was the dominant member of the family. His association with doctors raised hopes in him of an advance of the family into the ranks of the socially élite. He was a Mason, played golf, and mingled with a group of substantial citizens. Toward his family he was generous without being extravagant, and was inclined to be a little secretive about business affairs.

Mrs. Brown was an easy-going person, cheerful, inclined to give in, and devoted to her husband. She was never extravagant and did all her own work. A loving mother, she was contented with her lot and had no ambitions, as had her husband, to better their social status. She was a member of the Eastern Star but was inactive and found most of her social contacts in connection with two bridge groups, one made up of relatives.

The older daughter, Doris, had just finished 3 years at college. She was intelligent, generous, cheerful and dutiful toward her parents. Her objective was to be a Latin teacher. She was a member of a sorority, dressed well, and enjoyed the usual social activities of a college campus.

The younger girl, Harriet,* was perhaps a little more energetic than her sister, vivacious, enthusiastic about athletics. At this time she was a college freshman, a member of her sister's sorority, and enjoying herself immensely. Like her sister, she loved her home and was well satisfied with her lot.

The family organization was harmonious because all acquiesced in Mr. Brown's dominance.

Although the girls often aided their mother in the household tasks, they were encouraged always to prepare their lessons rather than help. The family did many things together—golf, bridge, and visiting friends and relatives. Joys and sorrows were shared with other members of the family and there was hearty co-operation in any family project. One of the unifying influences was the prospect of building a fine new house on the lot they had purchased. The girls were very proud of their parents and were happy to introduce their friends to them. Although the daughters had attended Sunday School until they were 13 or so, the family seldom went to church. Mr. and Mrs. Brown had tried to give their daughters every opportunity, and the girls appreciated it.

The depression cut Mr. Brown's business income down to about $1800 a year and his income from investments has almost stopped entirely. He is still the principal support of the family, however, for Doris, after graduating from the University of Michigan, to which she had transferred in her senior year, had succeeded only in securing a position as substitute teacher in the Chicago school system. This brings a very small and irregular income. The positions of family members are not, therefore, essentially altered.

The general effect of the decrease in income has been to increase the already strong solidarity. True, there are points of friction, but they are more than compensated for by the response to the challenge of family difficulty. Mr. Brown is not quite so cheerful as formerly and occasionally "blows up" over what he regards as needless expenditures. Doris has given up her plan for taking the Master's degree. The summer trip was abandoned, as has been the golf-club membership. Mr. Brown has given up his lodge membership and Mrs. Brown has dropped out of the Eastern Star. She likewise has given up the non-family bridge group. Doris and Harriet have cut down a great deal on clothes. Because they realize the family plight, both girls are more helpful at home and the younger has taken a more serious attitude toward her education. She is now at the University of Michigan. Mr. Brown no longer cherishes ambitions to break into higher social circles. Externally the family has kept up appearances, for the women still have their fur coats and Mrs. Brown cleans and presses Mr. Brown's suits herself.

Mutual helpfulness is shown by Doris' making clothes for her younger sister in her spare hours at home and Harriet's cheerful foregoing of an honorary sorority to which she had been elected and which she very much desired to join. The girls are greater pals than ever. Family objectives are more sedulously striven for than before. Harriet realized the seriousness of the family's economic plight when she discovered that her father had had to borrow money to keep her in college. She thereupon waged a successful campaign for the lowering of the sorority charges for room and board.

———

The Brown family seems quite typical of the Type I cases both in respect to original adaptability and integration. Likewise is it typical in showing itself firmly invulnerable to the pressure of a decrease with similar positions. The victory is hardly a victory at all because the contest is too one-sided. These families are prepared for this and more.

One of the interesting facts brought out in all eight cases representing the situation under discussion is that the challenge of the decrease awakened a greater sense of family unity than originally existed. This calls for explanation, since one might suppose that the phrase "firmly invulnerable" implies only the same degree of integration as originally existed. The truth seems to be that Type I families have latent powers which have not been fully called upon in the normal course of family life. They *have* the integration, but are not fully aware of it. When the decrease comes, it evokes these potentialities and the result is enhanced feelings of solidarity. Nor does this imply any shifts in member roles. The same structure becomes more self-conscious, if such a paradoxical expression may be permitted. Greater realization of family ties and family duties re-sults.

According to our conceptual framework there is no need that the conditions and incidents of the sociological process be similar in these eight cases, so long as the process itself is essentially so. How-ever, the families do happen to be quite alike in several respects. For instance, they were all fami-lies of business and professional men, their origi-nal incomes were high, but not so high as to make likely demoralization (between $5000 and $12,-000), and they lived in good-sized towns or cities. The percentage decrease in income was more divergent, varying from 50 per cent to 80 per cent. In four cases the father remained the only breadwinner. In one, a daughter had been work-ing before the decrease and continued to do so. In the remaining three, new members started working after the decrease, but in two of these (one of which is No. 32, given in full above), these members were just about to graduate from col-lege when the depression came and had intended to work anyway. The last case is that of a family in which the boy who was at college began to work for his board. (This is No. 40, used as the Type I example in Chapter II).

It is noticeable that the greater feeling of soli-darity after the decrease is mostly shown by greater willingness to do household tasks and help one another in a pecuniary way. This, after all, is to be expected, because it is chiefly in these directions that families which had a high standard of living did not need to show their strength before.

In all eight cases there is considerable worry in evidence after the decrease, especially on the part of the father. In some of them he is more irritable. His morale is nearly broken in one instance, Case No. 1, but the rest of the family has rallied to his help so well that the family organization is intact. Possibly this family could be regarded as readjustively invulnerable to this pressure rather than firmly so; at least it approaches that result more nearly than do the rest. In several cases the happiness of the family members has definitely decreased because of worry and the necessity of economizing. The mother in No. 43, for instance, will not buy new glasses, though she needs them badly. Special aspects of three of these cases, No. 1, No. 9 and No. 50 will be discussed further in Chapter XII.

Let us turn now to the Type I cases in which the decrease is accompanied, on the symbiotic level, by modified positions. There are three of these, and we will use No. 19 as their exemplar.

CASE NO. 19

The Rogers family consists of the parents and three children. At the time of the decrease the father was 45, the mother 41, a girl 17, and two boys, 13 and 1. They lived in a nice seven-room house for which they were paying in installments, on the outskirts of Grand Rapids. Although the furniture was not new, it was well cared for. Among the family's material possessions were a piano, radio, other musical instruments and a Chevrolet automobile.

Mr. and Mrs. Rogers were born and married in England but came to this country before their first child was born. Neither received much schooling in England and they therefore attended night school after coming here until they had obtained the equivalent of a high-school education. Mr. Rogers is a plumber by trade and was at this time employed pretty regularly by an established firm. He was a good husband and father, being particularly fond of playing with the baby. His principal associations were found through the local church, of which he was a charter member, and his trade. He turned over his earnings, with the exception of enough for gasoline and cigarettes, to his wife, and let her administer the family budget.

Mrs. Rogers' main interests were also her family and the church. She taught a girls' class in the Sunday School and attended church guild meetings. Her interest in her children led her to take an active part in the Parent-Teachers Association. Besides doing all her own housework, she made many of her children's clothes. One of her hobbies was gardening, and the yard was a constant source of enjoyment to her. She and her husband got along very well together and frequently visited friends in the evening.

The daughter, Margaret,* was at this time a high-school senior. She was fond of her studies, especially chemistry. Her chief recreations were music, swimming and tennis. She had earned money by giving music lessons, but she did not work in the summers, devoting herself rather to sports. Her close friends were few and she had no regular "gang." At this time she had three intimates—a boy at an Eastern university, a girl chum, and a somewhat older man who was a very fine musician. Margaret was inclined to be changeable in her moods—sometimes very gay, sometimes equally blue.

The 13-year-old boy, Wilbur, was of a different type—always happy-go-lucky and liked by every one. He was not fond of school and for a time had fallen in with rather undesirable companions. Mrs. Rogers and his teacher, however, managed to steer him away from them. He earned money by looking after the church lawn in the summer and tending the church furnace in the winter. His household chores consisted of helping his mother on Saturday mornings and cutting the lawn. He often brought friends home, much to his mother's delight. However, the other members of the family worried somewhat about his lack of seriousness. At this time a new interest in swimming was driving him to do better school work so that he would be eligible for the team.

The baby needs hardly any mention here except to say that he was the center around which the life of the family seemed to revolve.

The family still felt a strong sentimental tie with England, the baby having been named for King George. All their relatives still lived in England and there was much correspondence with them. The family had gone back for one visit before the birth of the baby.

Because of the very strict standards of the Rogers family, and because they did not wish their children to associate with vulgar boys and girls, some of the neighbors regarded them as snobbish. Mr. Rogers did not like to have the children out late and this was one of the chief sources of the little friction that there was in the family circle.

The two older children were friendly rivals in several respects—in seeing which could complete the allotted household chores first, in their music (one played the flute and the other the clarinet) and so on. There had been some jealousy of the new baby, but this was soon overcome.

The family co-operated on joint projects such as planting a new vegetable garden, painting the kitchen, and remodelling the attic. The evening meal was always a time for sharing the day's experiences and, just before retiring, the family had tea and toast, as the parents had been wont to do in England. Since all the family birthdays were in the same month, one big celebration was held which was always a memorable occasion.

Mr. Rogers knew that he could not send his children through college but he put aside what he could, and the whole family planned to achieve this end by the children helping one another.

The decrease came when Mr. Rogers was laid off by his employer, who decided to hire non-union men when hard times arrived. After that he tried to secure work as an independent plumber but could find almost nothing to do. In this emergency Mrs. Rogers secured three children who needed foster-home care and thus became the principal breadwinner. This introduced a difficult situation into the home, since it interfered considerably with normal family life.

This family presents, after the decrease, an unhappy spectacle, since all are much worried by the situation, but at the same time family ties have been knit even closer, for every member is concerned about the troubles of every other. The Rogers have had to accept fuel and even food from the welfare, and they are so far behind in their payments on the house that they fear they will lose it. Margaret has continued in college because she is self-supporting and would only be a burden at home.

66

The father has perhaps been hit the hardest. He has become much older and is very discouraged. His former employer has recently died, so that he has no chance of getting work at his old shop. He is trying to go it on his own with very little success. He works a little as a day laborer for the city. He spends his many leisure hours reading, waiting for calls.

Mrs. Rogers is now busier than ever with the three orphans to care for as well as her family. Church and garden are neglected. She is often very depressed, but hides it from the rest of the family.

Margaret was offered a four-year scholarship in a school in Grand Rapids and accepted it. She had to walk three miles every morning to eight-o'clock classes in order to save carfare. She is specializing in chemistry. She came to dislike the school and arranged through a friend for a job at the University of Michigan for the succeeding year.

Wilbur is still in high school, doing better in his studies, but considerably upset about his shabby appearance. He is also sensitive about the fact that he cannot entertain girls as the other boys do.

The family is more than ever a unit. Mrs. Rogers makes over clothes; Mr. Rogers and Wilbur repair things; the latter helps his mother more willingly than he used to; and Margaret tries to help by writing cheerful letters from college.

A quotation from this case is enlightening as a final word: "Sometimes our whole family gets so disgusted when we see other people wasting money in useless clothes, expensive food, cars and amusements while we could do so much good with it. I can always picture my mother saying 'Just think, they throw their money away as if it were coming in streams. And here we are, dying of thirst.' "

———

The Rogers family, and it is typical of Type I, shows itself readjustively invulnerable to the pressure of a decrease with modified positions. And moreover, this is an extreme case of modified positions; it could almost be classified as one of changed positions. What has happened is a smooth adaptation to the catastrophe, so that the family structure remains intact, though the family roles shift somewhat to correspond with the changed positions. It is interesting to note, however, that roles have not had to shift as much as the underlying positions because the mother was more or less the family leader in the first place.

The three families which belong here are rather similar in incidental conditions just as were those suffering a decrease with similar positions. The occupations of the father were that of plumber in No. 19, factory hand in No. 11,[1] and salesman in

[1] One aspect of this case was discussed in Chapter III and another aspect will be discussed in Chapter XII.

No. 29. Because in No. 29 the oldest boy, who was making a good income, contributed heavily to the family, the original income was considerably higher than the other two—$8600 as compared with $2700 and $2000. In this case the son continued to contribute after the decrease, but a much smaller amount. In the remaining two, other members had to go out and help earn the family's living. All three show slightly more feeling of integration after the decrease, not only on the symbiotic side, but in community of interests and affection as well. Thus they support the generalization that this type of family proves readjustively invulnerable to a decrease with modified positions.

Unfortunately we have only one Type I case coming under the pressure of a decrease with changed positions. This case, No. 4, is so unusual that it would be hazardous to draw general conclusions from it. As a human document, however, it is worth recording. No other family in our series has had such a complete change in its mode of life. It is classified as a highly adaptable one because there is every indication in the early situation that it would prove so. The fact that one member at least was unable to face the music does not warrant our changing the original type; and indeed the ultimate results point strongly to the correctness of the "highly adaptable" characterization.

CASE NO. 4

The Flemings were a family of four, living at the time of the decrease in a small Indiana town. Mr. Fleming was 49, Mrs. Fleming 43, Ralph 20, and Louise* 16. The maternal grandmother also made her home with them. Their house was one of the best in the community—a 10-room affair, with large verandas and a spacious lawn, worth more than $10,000. The family possessed a Ford, a piano, a radio and other musical instruments, as well as a fair-sized library. They were regarded as one of the leading families of the community.

Both Mr. and Mrs. Fleming had been born in this community and had lived there all their married life. Before his marriage Mr. Fleming had had notable success as a singer, travelling for 3 years in opera. He had then returned to his home community and settled down, becoming in turn a school teacher, superintendent, county clerk, county treasurer, partner in a Ford agency, and finally, full owner. He kept up his music and was known for his artistic talents as well as his community leadership. His net income was about $3000 a year.

"He was a good-looking man of Irish descent with blue eyes and black hair, intellectual face and pleasant smile, square shoulders, and springing step. His congenial social nature and joking pleasantry had won him the reputation of a good mixer.

He was sincere, of energetic nervous temperament, a quick thinker with common-sense ideas, a good sport, a considerate employer and an easy spender. He was particularly a man of high ambitions for financial success and a persevering, tireless worker—always putting in a great deal of overtime.

"Always holding a position requiring many social contacts, he became a leader in the community, actively interested in its educational, economic, and political welfare. His hobbies and recreational activities were mostly connected with his musical interests and included participation in neighborhood social gatherings, church activities, community musical entertainments and attendance at out-of-town operas. He also went on fishing and hunting trips and engaged in outdoor sports.

"Both his wife and children were very dear to him. No partiality was shown as between the two children, though he was perhaps inclined toward his daughter, who resembled him more. His chief incentive in his work was the success of his home life.

"He was not an extravagant spender, as the home and family were maintained out of his income without contracting bills. However, he was not stingy either, often sacrificing personal expenditures for the family's enjoyment, and he liked to maintain a certain standard of appearance in the home life. With his business funds he took more liberty of investment, taking out loans for its advancement, though careful in paying debts. Self-confident in his own ability to rise in the world, his philosophy was that life was what you made it."

Mrs. Fleming was "of similar Scotch-Irish descent, pretty, fun-loving, with brown hair and brown snappy eyes, a flashy smile of dimples and even teeth, and a well-kept athletic figure. A little reserved, but friendly, sincere, sympathetic and tactful. She was intelligent and capable, a woman of high ideals.

"Her experience had been limited but her outlook on life was wholesome, broad and cheerfully courageous. Coming from one of the poorer, but good families of the community, she had been a leader in her scholastic and social groups. She had had enough initiative to quit high school after her third year to aid in the family's support, and she held her position as a dry-goods store clerk until marriage. Through her married life she continued the habits of thrift and industry gained by her former experiences. With her children and family life her personality broadened and asserted itself in the community as definite leadership in the church and social clubs, with an active interest in education, politics, county child welfare, and a continuance of her own musical and literary education. Her recreations were of the family social type. Though particularly adapted to the friendly atmosphere of a small town, her interests were maintained above and beyond its narrowness.

"She too was vitally interested in her family life, though developing through it instead of bound to it. Though not partial in her guidance she perhaps inclined toward the boy who inherited her looks and disposition.

"Not stingy by nature, she was nevertheless a good manager, with her money, her time and her work. She had a great dislike for debts of any sort and preferred the financial security of a surplus to a high living standard or immediate pleasure. Her philosophy was perhaps to make the most of what life offered you instead of stretching after the unattainable."

Ralph, "with his mother's features, was always a bright, handsome chap. He lived the life of a normal boy through the grades, the neighborhood gang, Boy Scouts and Sunday School. He was a leader in the social and church life during his high-school years and prominent in extra-curricular activities. Always a good student and a hard-working boy at chores, extra jobs and vacation work, he was never particularly good in athletics, though of strong build. Self-confident through experiences such as short travel trips, above the average of children in the community, a little over-assertive, a big talker, he was pretty generally liked or at least accepted in the gang of his age group.

"He was interested in mechanical contrivances, and radio and telegraphic contraptions were his earlier hobbies. Later he took great interest in reading and poster-making, followed by considerable success as a saxophonist.

"Always saving of the slight income from Saturday jobs and vacation work, he had $400 worth of stock in his father's business at the finish of his high-school course.

"His friends were clean and wholesome, his own personal habits in regard to drinking, smoking and illicit relations were very good. He took pride in his home and home life, being perhaps a little closer to his mother during his high-school years. He had a healthy, impatient tolerance of his younger sister.

"In 1928 we find him in a college of small enrollment asserting the same qualities of sociability and leadership."

Louise* was "of Irish type, with black hair and blue eyes, fine features, oval intellectual face, small, athletic build, not beautiful but attractive looking because of dimpled smile, sweet but selfish disposition, energetic nervous temperament, a quick thinker and enthusiastic worker.

"Having an almost identical development through the grade and high school as the boy, though perhaps slightly more of the studious type, prominent in all community and school activities; holding minor jobs in summer and on Saturdays—

very thrifty with the income; taking interest in such activities as debate and piano, which widened her range of contacts. A girl of high ideals and conduct, liked by her own age group and elders, resting secure on her family's reputation, a little conceited over its position, and possessing a philosophy that life is limitless opportunity. Thus we find her in 1928 in her junior year in high school with a lot of family pride and egotism, with veiled admiration for the older brother and true affection for both parents, though perhaps in these few years leaning slightly toward the mother.

"The family's organization was as far as possible on a democratic basis. From infancy the two children were given a voice in control so as to teach them self-dependability and judgment—this voice extending more into domestic than economic life and relationships, and involving more self-government in that direction. Here the welfare of the group in preference to the welfare of the individual was the ruling policy and an open forum the judge and settlement of controversial questions.

"An equal division of the income between father and mother as well as small allowances to children and encouragement of any of their efforts toward financial independence, though slight, gave an economic unity and solidarity in the group.

"There was quite a bit of rivalry in school and musical achievement during grade and high school

75

between the two children, resulting sometimes in a conflict of personalities and occasionally in mutual co-operation. A few times they cliqued together against parents on some issue, though generally divided against each other. Occasionally they resorted to the old technique of petitioning the father through the mother, but due to his approachableness this was hardly ever necessary.

"The functions were allotted so that the duties of upkeep of car, home, and son fell to the father and the upkeep of furnishings, provision of food, and daughter's expenses fell to the mother, each providing their own personal expenses. The boy did the outside chores and the girl the inside—though neither were heavy.

"The family life was the centralizing force in the lives of all four members. No matter how diversified their interests and activities, nor how much and how long such interests and activities pulled each away from the group, there was always co-ordination and integration of the outside world in and through the home life. The specialized interests were brought into the group life to enrich and broaden the personality of each individual. Necessary to such integration was common interest in, and knowledge of, each individual's activities. Perhaps the best promoter of such a function was the meal-table discussion. Being a talkative family, the meals produced a practical forum of the day's activities; the father representing the financial news, political trends, down-town business men's ideas and gossip; the mother, the cultural news, current topics, neighborhood ideas and gossip; the two children, school life and newly acquired knowledge, one from the boy's viewpoint, the other from the girl's. Besides there were more general critical discussions of society at large through common participation in newpapers and favorite magazines.

"There were many activities in common, especially in the recreational field, such as community entertainments, neighborhood dances and parties, the theatre, out-of-town amusements, and short trips or picnic excursions, football games, eating out, etc.

"There was always a great to-do over Christmas, birthdays, April Fool's and St. Patrick's holidays. The Santa Claus, Christmas tree and Christmas morning surprises were traditions carried on past childhood into later group life. Birthdays meant dragging the favored one out of bed early for a group beating and a breakfast plate covered with presents. April Fool's day and St. Patrick's (due to Irish descent) were days of good humor and competitive mischief. A late Sunday breakfast, with church and company for dinner, was a usual practice. Many afternoon and evening concerts were joined in by all four. Joys were enthusiastically shared and there had fortunately been few sorrows. Such sadness as was caused by the death of friends and relatives was shared and not spared of the group."

The decrease, as it affected family positions, was, in the case of the Fleming family, a very complicated thing. We will have to consider the matter chronologically if we are to understand clearly. In 1923 Mr. Fleming had borrowed money to buy out the other partner in the Ford agency. For four years things went smoothly; the interest on this debt was paid, and the principal was gradually reduced. Then the Ford Company stopped making Model T in preparation for Model A. The new model was so long coming, that the overhead ate up all of Mr. Fleming's gains since 1923, so that he was worse off than when he started. He became so disgusted that he changed over to the Chevrolet, alas, just before the Model A finally came out. Although the business struggled along, Mr. Fleming could not regain the ground lost, and creditors began to hound him. At this time he started selling second mortgages on newly sold cars to the discount company without the knowledge of the owners, keeping up the payments out of new car sales. This policy would, of course, work only so long as new cars were being sold. Mr. Fleming tried to carry the whole burden of worry over the situation, being especially careful not to let the children know how precarious the family's position was. Mrs. Fleming knew in part the seriousness of the situation. She took in two school teachers as boarders to help out. But the strain was too great on Mr. Fleming. When he failed, in the spring of 1929, to secure an extension of a loan, he took $35 and a few personal belongings and left—for Canada. The business, of course, went into bankruptcy and a federal charge of defrauding through the mails was made against Mr. Fleming.

Mrs. Fleming took the blow courageously and soon obtained for herself a position as governess and maid in a millionaire's home in another state. The family home was turned over to the creditors, so that all the family had left was about $400. Louise lived with relatives that summer and entered college in the fall, drawing on the family's scanty reserves to do so until a bank failure wiped them out. Ralph secured a good summer position and became largely self-supporting for the rest of his college career. The next academic year both of the children received help from their mother, and the daughter received some from her father who was working as a lumberjack in Canada. The father decided to return and face the music, however, and went to prison in his home community to await trial. Six months later, though he pleaded guilty, he was given his freedom because of his past record and the petitions of friends. Two months later he obtained a salesman's job in another state, but it proved only temporary because of depression conditions.

Since the original catastrophe the family group has been together only twice, and they are now leading four separate lives though bound together by frequent correspondence.

Mr. Fleming is now "a man of 51, aged far beyond his years and could easily pass for 60. His hair is perfectly white, his eyes nearly gray, his face somewhat careworn though still genial. His shoulders are fairly drooped and his walk no longer is erect and elastic. His face and hands show the hardening effects of manual labor, his slight stoop, its strain. In company he continues his joking pleasantry, but is more moody when with a few intimates or alone. However, his outlook is still wholesome and hopeful though circumstances have taken away a lot of the poise resulting from self-confidence and have given him the viewpoint of a defeated man, beaten by life. Still energetic, capable, and a great worker, he dwells in a strange community looking for work, with no income.

"Due to his position and the lack of home life, what was once only a side line hobby is now becoming primary as a centralizing factor in his personality—his music. Strangely, his voice has held its own through these years. Music lessons, practice, and doing solo work in a large city church help to fill the time which would otherwise be dragging and full of worry in his search for work.

"His family letters are his chief joy—hoping through them to maintain the unity which was once so dear to him. His ambitions for financial success are no longer high but limited to an income which would sustain the group life once more and toward re-establishing that life his whole heart and soul are bent."

Mrs. Fleming, "now 45, is still very youthful in her appearance and bearing. Only 6 years younger than her husband she looks much more—enough to have been mistaken for his second wife. She has secured a job particularly suited to her ability and through it has gained even a greater social ease and breadth of outlook. As superintendent of a girls' orphan-home farm just outside a large city, she has opportunities for leadership, management, and social work far exceeding those of her past life. Financially independent, with expenses furnished and $100 a month salary, she is also the main financial stay of the family. Her experiences have kept her self-confident, her own nature has kept its fighting spirit of pluck and wholesome cheerfulness. However, she is more cynical in regard to the permanence of happiness and believes more in immediate pleasure than delayed joys.

"She is continuing her self-improvement and education through reading, constant contact with educational institutions and the broadening influence of city life. The children are her chief joy, though she has untied them from her apron strings and accepts the fact that the group will never be a social unit. However, her independence is lonely after having been surrounded by family love, and her desire for reunion with her husband is counter-acted only by her fear of dependency on her children."

Ralph, graduated from college, is now holding down a foreman's job in a big factory, far from the other members of his family. He is "very serious and mature for his age, also very hard and cynical, thinking life rather has it in for him and yet determined not to be downed. He attaches a predominant value to money and is not content to lead the life of the poor, but maintains a high standard of dress, food, and habitat at the expense of any financial surplus.

"He is still friendly and sincere, homesick for an environment of helpful encouragement and sympathy. He is still very much attached to his family and willing to fight for them, though pessimistic as to his father's chances. His character and conduct are still good, his ideals wholesome. He is still a little over-assertive and self-centered, but he is well-liked by his companions."

Louise, now a college junior, is "an energetic, hard-working student, though entering into many social and athletic activities with enthusiasm also. She is somewhat reserved and cold, skeptical as to the future, conservative and set in her opinions, a trifle self-centered. Though maintaining an average standard of dress, food and room on the allowance her mother gives her, her expenditures are chiefly for experiences which will broaden her personality such as concerts, entertainments and trips. She is sympathetic to the interest of the three others in the family and is sincere, helpful and encouraging in her contacts with them, though not particularly generous. She still feels that success can be won by sheer ability and that worth will finally come to the top. For that reason she is ambitious and optimistic as to the family's chances."

The Fleming's old friends and neighbors have not forgotten them, though none of the family lives in the old community, and they still admire them, not now for community leadership, but for the way they have met this crisis. As a consequence the family members feel the need of maintaining their individual integrity. Family pride is high on this new basis. The mother has assumed the true leadership of the family. She is merely a guiding hand, however, and in no way dominant. Co-operation and kindness among the family members is even more marked than before. A very active correspondence is kept up by each with all the rest, through which their experiences are still somewhat integrated. Family custom and ritual have little chance for expression and that only in a reminiscent way as in April Fool's letters and Christmas packages. The main thing that brings all member activities together "is that they are only different expressions of one objective—family integrity and financial security. Co-operation toward that goal is at present a consuming interest of all four."

———

Positions in the Fleming family are almost as radically changed as in any of the cases in our series. Certainly no other case shows greater role readjustments. And yet the structure of the group never broke. Even the father never lost his place in the family—only in the community. If one dared to generalize from one instance, one could conclude that Type I cases can surmount any difficulty arising from a decrease in income. They do not crack, no matter how severe their internal strains. Indeed it would almost seem as if the greater the shift in family positions, the more energies are called out to keep the family structure intact.

As I think back over the documents dealing with Type I families, a general picture is sketched in my mind. It is a picture of kindly, devoted parents and loving, if sometimes thoughtless, children. There is a good deal of common activity and mutuality of interest, coupled with not a little family ambition and pride. Yet this pride is not based on material possessions so much as upon the qualities of the members and the community recognition they have received. There is a stress upon homely virtues and a willingness to accept responsibility which presages success in meeting adversity. Such a family can take a decrease with similar positions in its stride, can readjust easily so as to surmount the obstacle of a decrease with modified positions, and, to all appearances, does not even falter at a decrease with changed positions.

CHAPTER V

HIGHLY INTEGRATED, MODERATELY ADAPTABLE FAMILIES

WE come now to families of the second type. These are similar to those discussed in the last chapter except that they are not characterized by the same degree of adaptability. The family as we originally observe it appears to be somewhat rigid as far as its potentialities for readjusting to a possible decrease in income are concerned. Usually this is manifested either by rather materialistic values, by irresponsibility in important family members, or by some formalism in family structure. Such qualities are not extreme in these cases, and the integration, of course, is just as strong as in the Type I families.

Unfortunately Type II families are sparsely represented in our series. Of the four such cases we have, two experienced a decrease with similar positions, and two a decrease with modified positions. The lack of any case showing a decrease with changed positions limits our ability to generalize about the reactions of this type, but extrapolation will enable us to hazard a guess or two.

Case No. 14 will serve to illustrate what happens when a Type II family encounters a decrease with similar positions, or, as we will sometimes call it, a simple decrease.

CASE NO. 14

The Kleins are a family of five—father, mother and three daughters, who, at the time of the decrease, were 15, 13 and 6. They were devout Jews who lived in one of the older residential sections of Columbus, a section which was just beginning to degenerate. The house was nicely furnished, but the exterior was not particularly prepossessing. The family was well able to afford a car, but did not have any at this time, because there seemed to be no particular need for one. The Kleins employed a maid and spent every summer at a resort, living rather well.

Mr. Klein was president of a well-established wholesale house and had an income of $6000 a year. Additional sums which he could have taken as profits if he had so desired were put back into the business. He had made numerous investments and provided a fund for the college education of each of his children. He was president of a branch of the state Credit Association. Personally he was pleasant, of high moral principles, conservative in his attitudes, and generous to those in need. His religion meant a great deal to him, and he was active in Jewish organizations. The general com-

87

munity charities also claimed his interest. He was an Elk, but most of his friends were Jews of about the same type as himself.

He allowed his wife to manage the household and held himself a little aloof. He used to bring home boxes of candy and other small luxuries to please the others. There was no favoritism, but he was very strict with the children.

Mrs. Klein took a more active interest in the family than did her husband. She had complete charge of the domestic budget. Her interests were not confined to her home, however, for she was interested in charities, took part in Temple plays, was head of the Sisterhood, played considerable bridge, and still found time to walk and read extensively. She was very impartial to the children and considerate of her husband.

Helen,* the oldest child, was obedient and studious. She went to religious school several times a week, took piano and elocution lessons, played tennis, went hiking, was a camp counsellor in handicraft, and was interested in high-school dramatics. She managed to save a little from her allowance of $1.50 a week, and with this she bought birthday gifts for her friends. Her associates were the children of her parents' friends. She fitted into the family well, though occasionally rebelling at the strictness of her parents.

Martha was in the eighth grade. She was a little more carefree than her older sister. Her

88

good nature and sense of humor won people. She was not saving and had a weakness for the small trinkets to be bought at the ten-cent store. Her interests were about the same as those of her older sister, and she was a healthy, happy child.

The youngest girl was just beginning school. Her playmates, unlike those of her sisters, were just neighborhood children, not necessarily of the Jewish faith. As was natural, she received more than her share of the parents' attention, but her sisters were not jealous.

The mother was the real leader of the family group, the father being somewhat apart. There were no particular functions for the children to perform in the home. Family solidarity was chiefly shown in the family religious observances. All the holidays were celebrated and the Sabbath was observed together. The discipline in the family was inclined to be cruel—whipping being not uncommon. Yet the childern bore no lasting resentments and the family was really closely knit.

The sincere interest of the parents in their children was shown by the opportunities they afforded them—dancing, piano and elocution lessons, and Girl Scout membership. Indeed these activities sometimes became burdensome to the girls, but the parents were determined that the children should take advantage of them and insisted upon their participating.

The business began to slow up in 1927 and the

family income was finally cut almost in half. No change in positions took place, the father remaining the sole wage earner and the mother continuing in charge of the home.

Mr. Klein has been the one most severely affected by the decrease. Though his integrity and sincerity have remained intact, at first he lost his mental poise, became very pessimistic and finally had to consult a psychiatrist before he could carry on his work. This treatment has worked a great change in his personality, so that he is now chiefly interested in self-expression, where he formerly accepted as fundamental the obligations imposed by his religion. He has also regressed in the direction of dependence on his mother. His affiliations are now much less close with the Temple. He no longer pays dues to the Elks, but as a new diversion is playing a little golf. He also does more reading than he formerly did. His taste for fishing trips has declined; he likes more lively entertainment. He is more open-handed with the less money he has, loving to surprise the rest of the family by bringing home something new, such as a radio. He is still very much absorbed in his business.

For a while there was considerable strain between Mr. and Mrs. Klein because he took the attitude that part of their difficulty was due to the fact that he had given her too exclusive control over the budget, and she resented the implication.

These elements of friction have been smoothed over now.

The mother was not bothered much by the decrease. She has been very much upset over Mr. Klein's defection from Judaism, however. The children also do not seem to have been affected much. Economies have been brought about by hiring a cheaper maid, foregoing the redecorating of the house and eliminating vacations, economies which have not really cut deep with the children. Helen has been able to continue in college by reason of the fund which had been set aside for that purpose.

The decrease has brought Mr. Klein closer to his children. "He has made his paternal love more than an abstraction. He has taken a very definite interest in the children's interests and in the mother's activities. In turn he has shared his confidences and his cares, thus bringing the rest of the family more closely in alliance with him and with each other." Leadership is shared by both parents now and the mother has willingly ceded part of her former primacy. The parents are not so strict as formerly. Whippings are no longer administered, even to the youngest daughter.

There is more family life and more common activity. The family spends many evenings playing anagrams together. Jewish customs have been continued but the father participates in these more to please his wife than from conviction.

Joys and sorrows are fully shared. "It has been a feeling of a common burden of father's care and worries that made the situation a great deal easier to bear."

Most of the opportunities afforded the children have been continued—lessons of various kinds in particular.

———

The reason for regarding the Klein family as highly integrated but only moderately adaptable is that there seems to have been a strong family sense, probably due in part to religious influences, and a good deal of unity, while at the same time the pattern was one of authoritarian discipline and was dictated by traditional views. This absence of democracy looked like a weakness right from the start. The immediate reaction to the decrease in the way of strain and friction, followed later by a more integrated adjustment, is found in several other cases.

The only other case comparable to this one is No. 6. It reveals the rather similar experiences of a well-to-do mechanical engineer's family in a small Indiana town. The moderately adaptable rating in this instance was given because of the high standard of living coupled with the children's strong desire for material possessions. On the whole, however, the family rose to the challenge and a more helpful attitude developed than had existed before.

When one compares the reaction of a Type II family to a simple decrease with that of a Type I family, one feels that the latter stands up better. The greater original adaptability seems to cause greater sureness and power when the blow of the decrease strikes. The Type II families have more trouble in maintaining their solidarity, though they manage to do so successfully.

Our evidence concerning the effect of a decrease with modified positions upon a Type II family is interesting because it is conflicting. One of the families holds its own, while the other appears vulnerable. We will take the one which yielded under the pressure, No. 53, as our example.

CASE NO. 53

The Schiller family at the time of the decrease consisted of the father, aged 43, mother, 37, girls of 18 and 12, and boys of 17, 14 and 6. They lived in a small Michigan town where Mr. Schiller was a banker. As befitted his community position, the family had one of the nicest and largest houses in town. It was equipped with all modern conveniences such as an electric stove and an electric clothes drier, and the family owned an automobile and a radio. Mr. Schiller's income was about $5000 a year prior to the decrease.

He was "a man of frail physique but he possessed an infinite amount of nervous energy."

93

Cautious in his business dealings, he was more impulsive at home. He was alert and inquisitive. He was a devout church member. His friends were few and most of his leisure hours were spent with the family or working about the home. "For a man of strong religious and ethical prejudices he was extremely tolerant in his attitude toward other members of the family." He did not seem to make a favorite of any of the children.

Mrs. Schiller was very domestic. Her whole life centered in her home and her children. "She enjoyed being a comfort and a help to her husband, she enjoyed rearing her children, she enjoyed housework and she desired nothing more than that she might do these things." She possessed a remarkable degree of tact and understanding, but was not particularly capable in other ways. She was completely dependent upon her husband for her ideas and attitudes outside of her home sphere. She never made any expenditures without the consent of her husband.

Gertrude,* the oldest child, was a bright, studious type, inclined to be a little pessimistic. Her hope was to become a teacher of higher mathematics. She seemed to be less than normally interested in the opposite sex. Only with reluctance did she participate in the activities of the family group, and, with the exception of her father, with whom she liked to discuss economic problems, merely tolerated the other members of the family.

94

Raymond, the oldest boy, had the frail physique of his father but the personality of his mother. He was a good mixer, his associates consisting of all sorts of people, from social outcasts to the socially élite. He had transient enthusiasms for literature, art, and music. He was the most extravagant member of the family and was always trying to get his allowance increased. The others were fond of him because of his tact and his willingness to do things with them.

Frederick, the 14-year-old boy, was a normal type of lad whose interests were not chiefly scholastic, but were centered in his neighborhood gang and in tinkering with mechanical devices. He was not particularly close to the rest of the family.

Margaret, 12 years old, was a typical tom-boy. She was constantly in the open air, romping, playing ball, climbing trees. She was large for her age and extremely healthy. Her only domestic duties were to help in looking after her younger brother. She was tolerant and good humored and not nervous, like the other children.

Herbert, aged 4, was an ordinary but rather spoiled child. He demanded constant and immediate attention in the family group and got it.

The German heritage of the family tended to keep it unified, for family pride and the enjoyment of group activities were strong. The family rather fancied itself as more intellectual than most middle-class families and more substantial in their inter-

95

ests and activities than "society" people. The Schillers always went to church as a group, and all holidays and birthdays were celebrated. A typical Christmas day: "The usual preparation was made, such as the buying of gifts and the decorating of the tree. On Christmas Eve every one hung up his stocking and all but the parents went to bed. At exactly eight o'clock the next morning my father would tap on the bedroom doors, wishing each person 'Merry Christmas' and telling each to get up and dress while he went downstairs to see if 'Santa has been here.' Soon he would return with a look of suppressed excitement on his face and say, 'Well, it looks as if he remembered us all right.' Next all seven of us would march down the stairway in single file, the youngest going first and my father bringing up the rear. The gifts were then distributed by my father. At nine-thirty a buffet breakfast was prepared and every one dressed for church. Most of the afternoon was taken up with the huge chicken dinner and the evening was spent in reading stories aloud in the living-room. This procedure was performed exactly on every Christmas day. I think this illustration shows that my family possessed a strong sense of 'we' since these common activities and rituals were always performed with the greatest enjoyment and pride. No member of the family ever thought of not taking part in these common

has become very frugal but at the same time he does not wish the family to lose any really worthwhile opportunities and values.

"My mother seems to thrive under the new conditions imposed upon her. She has taken the place of my father in family affairs, she has become the leader in the struggle for adjustment." She is very firm in enforcing economy on the children, more despotic than her husband ever was. She has maintained her optimism in the face of her husband's pessimism and has heartened the rest of the family.

Gertrude has had 2 years at college where she is working for her room and board. She is studying to teach mathematics. Her interest in the family has increased and she is trying to repay their sacrifices for her by being as helpful as she can.

"Raymond is attending college also, but only because he has not been able to adjust himself to the change in family life. His habits, personal tastes and interests are expensive ones and he has never learned to do anything which could be called useful work. His presence at home was considered harmful because he could not be made to conform to the necessary prohibitions which the decreased income demands; family pride would not allow his parents to disown him and so they have put him in school and let him get along as well as he can on the little money which they can send him. He has assumed a disinterested, 'Oh, what the hell' attitude toward life in general and toward the members of the family in particular. His friends are cheap and unintelligent, and because of loose habits his health is failing rapidly.

"After 1931, Frederick began to develop into a tall, nervous youth whose interests are entirely self-centered. His attitude toward the other members of the family is absolute unconcern unless he is approached by one of them, when he will usually become peevish and very often fly into a fit of rage. He has become intensely interested in scientific subjects of all sorts and is continually puttering about a small workshop which he has constructed himself and outfitted with money which he has earned by doing odd jobs. Although he resents interruptions and intrusions upon these activities, he will usually, after a good deal of grumbling, comply with the requests or demands of his parents. He seems to have a great admiration for his older brother and will often come to him for advice and appreciation."

Since the decrease Margaret has shown a remarkable willingness to assume domestic responsibilities. Her interests center wholly in the realm of violent physical activities and she has expressed a desire to become a physical education teacher. Toward other members of the family she is always helpful and sympathetic and is a constant source of amusement and cheer.

Even Herbert, young as he is (6), realizes that

some drastic change has taken place in the family fortunes. He listens closely to all family discussion and, because they usually concern matters of finance, has developed a great desire to earn money. As a result he has become the originator and promoter of numerous business ventures in his play group.

The family is not so certain as it formerly was of its superiority to other middle-class families. The delight in group activities has quite largely disappeared. Because the mother is closer to Margaret, Raymond, and Herbert, her rise to dominance has tended to form a clique with Mr. Schiller, Gertrude, and Frederick in the opposite camp. "There is a proud sense of 'we' in the family still but it is objective rather than subjective, that is, not 'we are a happy, prosperous and industrious family,' but 'we must appear to be a happy, prosperous and industrious family.' "

———

The validity of regarding the Schillers as originally a highly integrated family is hardly open to question, but one might well wonder at our moderately adaptable characterization. The fact is that this family exhibited several features, no one of which alone would put it in this category, but which taken together seem to compel this classification. Three things particularly stand out; a strong German heritage, which often spells stubborn resistance to change; Mrs. Schiller's complete dependence on her husband, which would make new arrangements difficult; and Raymond's spendthrift inclinations.

This case is particularly interesting because the modification of positions does not entail any change in the actual bread-winning activities. The alteration is in the control of the spending budget and is due to the father's preoccupation with his business. This was nevertheless an immediately practical adjustment, not a secondary, attitudinal one and therefore deserves to be included as part of the impinging pressure of the decrease. The family would never have made this arrangement if it had not been forced to, because Mrs. Schiller had hitherto been so dependent in these matters.

The results invite comment and encourage speculation. We see here a family upon the members of which the decrease has had very different effects. Some are more devoted to the whole than before, some considerably less so. Perhaps we might argue that this shows the original integration to have been weak, though it looked strong, and that there really was little structure capable of resisting pressure. At all events the family's behavior is prophetic of that of the unintegrated families in Types VII and VIII.

The other similar case, No. 49, is the family of a good-natured but rather old-fashioned pharmacist, a family which was characterized as moderately adaptable precisely because he seemed to be rather weak and ineffectual. In this instance the modified positions came about by the mother securing a job which gave her an income equal to that of her husband, though the organization of the family was not radically changed. Unlike the case we have just reviewed, No. 49 proved invulnerable to the pressure and came out a more consciously integrated family than it was originally.

How are we to explain the differing results of two families of the same type under the same pressure? There are at least two possible ways of doing so. Perhaps our type system is too crude, so that essentially different kinds of families, with different degrees of vulnerability, are to be found in the same type. If this is the case, we may hope that further research will indicate just what refinements of our technique are needed to discriminate such differences. It does not seem likely that it will merely prove to be a multiplication of categories on the same basis that we have at present, for No. 49 seemed to have no superiority in integration, adaptability or lightness of the impinging pressure over No. 53.

Another possible explanation is that the modified positions situation represents the critical point for Type II cases, so that, when they encounter this pressure, they act in an indeterminate way, some falling to one side, some to the other. This interpretation is scientifically less satisfactory than the former one, for it is practically an acquiescence in defeat. It is, to go back to our analogy of the buildings, like admitting that we do not know and cannot find out why, of two apparently similar structures subjected to exactly the same wind, one falls down and the other does not. Surely this confession should be made only after exhaustive study of all the particulars of a large number of such instances, and this has not yet been done for families experiencing a decrease in income.

The fact here seems to be that the modifications of position required modifications of role. Case No. 49 had the capacity for a steady and effective readjustment of roles; Case No. 53 did not. The difference was probably due to obscure psychological factors in the Schiller family which the case history, though a thorough one, did not reveal. Undoubtedly if all these factors had been known, the family would have been classified either as belonging to Type III, Type V, or even Type VI.

We hinted above that we might be able to extrapolate so as to guess how a Type II family would react to a changed positions decrease. In view of the evidence of the Schiller family and of the general tendency for Type II families to meet the problem less effectively than Type I families confronting similar conditions, I am inclined to believe that a Type II family would prove vulnerable to the pressure of a decrease with changed positions. When we see how other types behave under various conditions this guess will be shown to have substantial circumstantial evidence to support it.

The general picture one gets from the four Type II cases is not so consistent as that obtained from the Type I families. This is probably because the weaknesses in adaptability take different forms. As far as the circumstances and characteristics of family life are concerned, these families have little in common except their similar degree of integration. When you have said that in all of them the parents are deeply interested in the welfare of their children and that there is considerable common activity involving both parents and children, you have said almost everything that can be said. The mediocre adaptability does not prevent this type of family from being firmly invulnerable to a simple decrease and it seems probable that most of them would prove readjustively invulnerable to a decrease with modified positions. Our hypothesis for the present, however, is that Type III families could not stand the strain of a decrease with changed positions.

CHAPTER VI

HIGHLY INTEGRATED, UNADAPT-ABLE FAMILIES

In a small number of families one would expect to encounter few belonging to Type III, because to become well integrated in the changing complexities of modern life almost requires adaptability. The two cases in our series which seem originally to belong to this type are, interestingly enough, both of immigrant heritage. They had both maintained a strong unity previous to the depression probably because of remoteness from the changing forces of modern life. One family lived in the country, while the other was well established in one of the immigrant groups in a large city. Their unadaptability arose mainly from the father in each case. In the rural family he was irresponsible, in the city family, very dogmatic, stubborn and domineering. It is fortunate that these two families experienced the same kind of decrease, a decrease with no change in positions, for this gives our generalizations more weight than would be the case where each one stood alone. A natural scientist will not accept the results of an experiment unless it is done at least twice. How much more reason for caution in the undeveloped field of social science!

Since we will wish to consider Case No. 47 **in** Chapter XII because of certain special features connected with it, we will use Case No. 23 as our illustration here.

CASE NO. 23

At the time of the decrease the Majeski family consisted of the parents, both 45, a girl 16, and a boy 13. They lived on a farm, but Mr. Majeski did not work it. Instead he rented it out and drove daily to work as foreman in a factory in a town about 25 miles distant. The home was a new, modern frame house, with furnace heat and bathroom. It was comparatively well furnished and the family owned a piano, victrola, and radio, as well as the small car in which the father drove to work. The family kept a cow and some poultry and had a small vegetable garden to supply household needs. On the whole, the home was very attractive for a rural one.

Both Mr. and Mrs. Majeski were born in Chicago, of immigrant parents. They lived in that city for 10 years after their marriage and then came to this farm. They had retained little of the European culture heritage possessed by their parents and considered themselves simply middle-class Americans.

Mr. Majeski's yearly income was about $1700. He was a steady worker, but by no means energetic or dynamic. His philosophy was to take things easily and let matters slide, if possible. He had never tried to save money for a rainy day and at this time was counting rather heavily on an inheritance of $10,000 or $15,000 which he might receive any time. If the budget would balance until then he was satisfied. He had great hopes of his children "getting ahead." One of his avocations was keeping his new home up to date. His friends were close and few. Though a lodge and church member, he was not active in either. His interests were simple and inexpensive—radio listening and tinkering, riding, smoking, an occasional friendly game of cards. He had almost no civic interest and rarely read anything but the daily paper. His attitude toward other members of the family was tolerant, almost indifferent. He seldom intervened with the children, but when he did, it was to give a sharp, short and final reprimand.

Mrs. Majeski was quite different from her husband. She was the worrying, nervous, sentimental kind, and literally lived for her children. There was not the greatest co-operation between her and her husband. She was thrifty and always concerned about the future, taking a paternalistic attitude toward the children, whereas Mr. Majeski could not be bothered with cares of this kind. She begrudged the little time which her club and church activities took away from her home, for she considered child rearing her sacred obligation. She would willingly have worked to help the family to a higher standard of living, but the husband would have none of this because he considered such a step a reflection upon his ability to support his family, an ability of which he was very proud. The children respected their mother more than they did their father, because of her interest and sympathy for them.

Frances, just graduated from high school at this time, suffered from chronic poor health. She was sensitive about this and had feelings of inferiority. Her success in high school had not been marked and the family did not therefore think it worth while to send her to college. At the same time she had a strong sense of responsibility and did not like being a parasite at home. Her dominant interest was her church work. She was retiring and had few, but close, friends. She tended to be reserved with other members of the family.

Harold was quite the opposite from his sister. He had an optimistic, cheerful attitude toward life and had no desire to take on responsibilities. Those which he recognized he took seriously, however. He was popular and had many friends, though no close ones. He was not careful in regard to expenditures and his mother had to watch him constantly relative to this. His chief interest seemed to be to have a good time. Shows, dates and auto rides were indulged in every night he could "get away." His considerable success in school work led to feelings of superiority, and this threatened to hurt his progress because he thought his natural quickness was a substitute for industry. His hobbies centered about church and school social activities—athletics, debating, dramatics, and parties. He was not inclined to talk about his personal affairs at home. His mother worried about this, but not his father.

"The personal relations of the members of the family were harmonious, but not exactly ideal. The father assumed undisputed leadership in business and financial affairs, but was watched very closely by the mother because he was so careless. In the rearing of the children and the management of the household the mother assumed not only leadership but sole responsibility. These two spheres were pretty well marked out and seldom was there any trespassing. There was always complete frankness, but not always understanding.

"It was always felt that the children should have some work to do, and the numerous chores around the little farm were suited to the purpose. There was a tendency for the children to shirk the responsibilities of their chores, which were then assumed by the mother. On the whole, though, there was a high degree of harmony, if not such a high degree of efficiency.

"The solidarity of the family was quite complete. The majority of the play interests were activities and none considered them silly or sentimental."

The parents tried to train the children to respect one another's views, aspirations and feelings. If there were signs that this was not being done, the father would first reproach the offending member kindly, then warn him, and finally compel conformity by withdrawing privileges and stopping the allowance.

The children were not forced to take advantage of opportunities, but were allowed to go more or less their own way at their own speed. The father was the one who enforced discipline and set down whatever limitations there were. He was particularly concerned with health, and insisted upon early retirement and abstention from tobacco and alcohol.

The modification of positions, brought about by the decrease, occurred in this way: So preoccupied did Mr. Schiller become with the bank and its problems that he gave over all control of the household to Mrs. Schiller. She was unused to this and it made the problem of adjustment more difficult.

Mr. Schiller has narrowed the range of his interests since the depression. His business and his Sunday School class seem to be the only things beside his family to retain any hold on him. His income is down to about $2000. He is worried, a little impatient and touchy, sometimes sullen. He shared by the whole family. Visits were made largely by the family as a whole, not individually. The interest in the beauty of the home and grounds was a mutual one. Church interests were another set of mutual interests. The several interests identified with the car—Sunday afternoons, rides, picnics, outings, were mutually shared. Radio listening was a family activity. If one was obliged to stay away from one of these he felt apologetic.

"Sometimes personal desires were deliberately sacrificed to aid another." Not infrequently this was done foolishly, and highly important interests sacrificed for less significant ones. "There seemed to be an inability to see first things first. In summary, it might be said that the 'we' feeling was intense, and co-operation in the attainment of individual desires quite complete, but that there seemed to be little discrimination between worthy and less worthy activities with the result that the opportunity to gain the maximum advantage from the co-operation was not realized as it might have been."

The decrease in income has come from two sides—a reduction in the father's wage rate and his hours of work, and a falling off in the rent from the farm. The family income is now about $1200. No significant changes in member positions accompanied this decrease.

The father is affected the least. He is not alarmed, but he is a little more concerned about the future than before. "He resents the fact that there is friction in the family concerning financial matters—a concern which he cannot conceive of as being so very important. He spends more time away from home. He is annoyed by the fact that the home needs painting, that it is time to trade the car in and he can't afford to pay the balance, and that creditors are becoming increasingly obnoxious. He still refuses to let his wife assist in supporting the family, though she has had the opportunity to do so several times. He refuses to recognize the fact that expenses have to be curtailed or a crisis will result. He meets the new situation by cowardly denying its existence."

The mother is "becoming more nervous, more worried, more hard working. Her associations with outside groups are declining in frequency. Her paternalistic attitude toward her children is *increased to the breaking point.* She is annoyed by the indifferent attitude of her husband and decries the increased debt and the run-down condition of the home, and points out again and again that this cannot go on forever. Relations between her and her husband are strained. She has become a 'nagging wife,' but she feels that she is a 'prophet crying in the wilderness.' She is losing the respect of her children but she doesn't seem to see it."

Frances is doing what she can to help meet the situation, but her expenditures were so few before that she cannot save much. She is conscious of the growing antagonism between her father and mother and is trying to assume the role of mediator without much success. She feels she has alienated the affection of both in the attempt. Her interests are less in the church, more in the home. Her reading interests are absorbing more and more of her time and she is becoming almost a recluse. Brooding over her parents' friction has had something to do with this. "Her friends are fewer because she has less time to spend with them and is less interested—and undoubtedly much less interesting."

"Harold 'suffers' from a lack of spending money. His mother, being his supervisor in this respect, not only curtails his spending money but lectures him concerning the financial status of the family. He fails to see any need for curtailing expenses and his father quite agrees with him. He can't have so many 'dates' and shows nevertheless. He blames his mother for these inconveniences and is becoming more and more secretive. While his spending money is cut, he spends more *time* away from home. His whereabouts are less known, and are much less desirable for a high-school boy. He is becoming less and less inclined to assume his allotted functions around the home and farm. School and church interests are still dominant, but they are slipping. On the whole he is less concerned with worthy things."

The father's control over fiscal matters is no longer undisputed. He resents the challenge strongly and considers it a pernicious personal criticism. Mrs. Majeski "doesn't relish the idea of conflict, but feels that she must use whatever influence she has in an effort to convince the family of the folly of refusing to adjust. The mother has ceased to be the advising agency for the children, partly because of her increasing inability to sympathize, which is mistaken for increased indisposition to sympathize." A feeling of distrust hovers over the home.

"Superficially the solidarity of the family would seem to be maintained. Actually it is threatened. Habitually many of the old play interests go on, but the old vigor seems to be lost. A Sunday afternoon ride in the car ceases to be a mutual joy when one member of the group is watching the mounting mileage with visions of service station bills. Participation is merely habitual—not actually voluntary and spontaneous any longer. Group activities with which there is no great cost connected are still shared quite completely. Church activities are still quite absorbing family interests, as is also visiting."

The results in the Majeski family lead naturally to the hypothesis that a highly integrated, but unadaptable family is vulnerable even to the pressure of a simple decrease. This hypothesis is con-

firmed by our other case in Type III, No. 47. Here
the failure to cope with the situation was not so
clearly evident, but the family certainly did not
come through unscathed. The critical pressure for
this type is evidently a slight one, and we may
therefore conclude that decreases with modified
and changed positions would only have shown even
more marked vulnerability.

This type well illustrates a proposition which
will become more evident as we go further: adaptability is more important for meeting a decrease
than integration. After all this is only common
sense. It is a change which is causing the pressure,
and cohesiveness would necessarily play a second
fiddle to flexibility. The morale of an army march-
ing in close column can always be broken by am-
bushed enemies if it persists in its suicidal for-
mation, and perhaps it makes little difference how
much group feeling the units have when the attack comes.

We may sum up our treatment of Type III by
stating that conditions of modern life probably
make this type of rare occurrence; that families out
of the main curents of modern life are particularly
likely to fall here; that the high integration cannot
make up for deficiency in adaptability when it comes
to meeting a decrease; and that these families are
therefore bad risks when confronted with a depression situation.

CHAPTER VII

MODERATELY INTEGRATED, HIGHLY ADAPTABLE FAMILIES

TYPE IV is well represented in our series with nine families. Because of the greater importance of adaptability, their reactions are more similar to Type I than to either Type II or Type III and we shall see that they stand the strain very nearly as well. Of the nine, seven underwent a simple decrease, and one each a decrease with modified positions and with changed positions. Our illustrative case for a moderately integrated, highly adaptable family reacting to the pressure of a decrease with similar positions is No. 13.

CASE NO. 13

The Haywood-Jones family represents the union of two formerly independent families. Mr. Haywood had two children by his first wife who died, and some years later he married Mrs. Jones, a widow, who brought with her into the family her own two children. Thus at the time of the decrease there were two brother-sister sets of children living together. Mr. Haywood was 47, Mrs. Haywood 45, Robert Haywood* 20, Jane

Haywood 16, Mary Jones 20, and Peter Jones, 17. We find, then, the unusual situation of four children between 16 and 20 in the same family group.

The family lived in one of the better middle-class residential districts of Jackson, Michigan. Their house was of frame construction, contained seven rooms, and was modern in its equipment "from radio to refrigerator." The family possessed an Oldsmobile, and a canoe, row boat and outboard motor for their vacations. The well-kept yard was adjoined in the rear by a vacant lot not belonging to the Haywoods but which the owner was glad to have them use as a flower and vegetable garden.

Mr. Haywood was in the insurance business and had recently been transferred from the office force to the selling side, so that at this time he was on the road a good deal. His income was $5000. "Being a real business man he kept close tab on all income and outgo and the end of each month regularly saw him at his desk going over all his bills, receipts, check stubs and bank balances.

"His energy has always seemed boundless; never too tired to do a little bit of extra work or play. Temperamentally he was usually serene, but on occasions would fly into momentary anger or have short fits of worry. He was never easy-going or careless, but was prone to allow the children to have their way after a short argument unless he was sure their wishes were absolutely detrimental.

His cheerful and optimistic outlook on life and all its problems endeared him to every one, but he never let this attitude overrule his sound common sense, of which he seemed always to have more than his share or more than his slight education would ordinarily indicate. Although only having a little better than a tenth-grade education, through extensive reading and constant application to learning what he could at every opportunity, his manner, speech and ability were far superior to those of many college graduates. His openness and sincerity had gained him many friends and had always been a big help to him in his desire to do the best he could. Although a man of middle age, he, before the decrease, had always kept himself young in spirit and appearance through his love of the outdoors and his liking for fishing, swimming, sailing, camping, and golf. Besides the many hours spent in these activities he loved to putter away an extra hour or two every chance he got during the spring and summer in gardening; the things that would most swell him with pride were a heavy 22-inch rainbow [trout—*Ed.*] or a crop-heavy garden.

"Being of a very friendly nature, his friends were of all types, races, and creeds; money or social position had no bearing on his choice in this matter; as long as a man was frank, clean, sincere, human, and an all-around 'good fellow' he was eligible to be a friend. In business he had always steered far from the narrow-minded, petty or dishonest types and picked men for associates who were looked up to in the community; that is, bankers, lawyers, store owners, etc. In dealing with the family he was always as fair as possible and did his best to settle disputes in a just way. About his only wavering in absolute justice was his tendency to favor his own son, Robert, but this was natural, for during the period of his widowerhood he had chummed with his son in all spare moments. As far as the stepchildren were concerned, contrary to general belief, he and they were more real father and children than some of the natural families of our neighborhood. Mr. Haywood's main ambition had always been to provide amply for the comforts of his family and to see that the children got a better prepared start in life than he did."

Mrs. Haywood was "a woman of medium height, slightly thin, who, although always apparently in good health, continually contended that she was unwell. She was nervous and quite irritable in temperament and subject to frequent outbursts of flaring temper, but still a good mother, wife and homemaker; full of the usual energy of a nervous person and always digging around the house to find extra work to do, at the same time complaining of how she felt and how she ought not to be working so hard. Outside of her complaining over her physical condition she looked upon life as a happy game, and always obtained the maximum of pleasure possible; serious in her desire to make a good home for her husband, children and stepchildren, a good manager, and "good sport," but inclined to be tyrannical and domineering with the children. Her desire for further education was greatly enhanced by her second husband—so far as to make her take up extensive reading and classes in foreign language in night school, and they always enjoyed a spirit of competition in doing their assignments and becoming proficient in their subjects. Her second marriage also affected her recreational life; previously, shows, cards and other such amusements took up her spare time, but, since, she had become intensely interested in her husband's hobbies—fishing, camping, motoring, and outdoor life. Besides the family, she had many friends, but only a few close ones, these being old school chums of about her own age. Even these she went about with very little, an occasional show or drive, and never to bridge parties or other social functions. Her attitude and relations with the family, especially her stepchildren, was always far superior to the average belief about stepmothers, and, although jealous of Robert's hold upon his father, seldom verbally or otherwise showed it to members of the family other than Robert himself. This often came in the form of disputes between the two— generally of a verbal character, but a few times going so far as to obtain Robert a round of good sound slaps. Her favoritism showed up once in a while in overlooking pranks of her own son that the stepson would have been scolded or even punished for, but on the whole her treatment of the entire family was quite fair and unbiased."

Robert (Haywood) was at this time a normal, healthy, energetic and restless but not robust boy, who was easy-going and happy most of the time, but who lapsed into moodiness occasionally. He was capable enough mentally but rarely applied himself, a great "starter" but a mediocre "finisher." He was friendly to all and affectionate toward his intimates. He liked to be the head of whatever he was in and was perhaps a bit conceited. He had spent most of his time during high school in extra-curricular and social activities of all kinds. He spent as much of his leisure time as possible with his father, and in the summer they were constant companions, swimming, boating, and fishing. After taking one year of junior college he had gone to work as an engineering draftsman in Detroit, where he learned to be more careful of money than he had been before. He had wanted to enter the University of Michigan but his father had refused to give him the money, because he felt that the boy needed to acquire a more serious attitude. Robert's friends were of the middle class, of good family and sound morality. He detested snobs. His family attitudes were: a comradeship with his father; a devotion to his own sister, Jane; smooth-flowing friendship with his stepbrother and sister; and mingled feelings toward his stepmother. He had naturally resented somewhat the second marriage because it encroached upon his companionship with his father.

Jane was in the tenth grade in high school at this time. She was calm, cheerful, witty, easy to get along with. An honor-roll student, she yet found time to devote to tennis, swimming, and clubs. She was a willing worker and for this reason was quite often imposed upon by other members of the family in regard to household duties. She had many friends, mostly of respectable middle-class families, more girls than boys. She was thrifty, but always managed to be smartly dressed. She got along well with all members of the family, since the only disagreements arose from her dislike of camping trips and fishing.

Mary Jones was a good-looking, healthy girl with a tendency toward plumpness, who was inclined to complain about her health, like her mother. Lively enough when fun was in prospect, she was lazy and inefficient in carrying out her duties. Easy-going, happy-go-lucky, easy to get along with when not crossed, she was stubborn and nasty when opposed. She was bright enough intellectually and a pleasant companion. Through lack of application she was a mediocre student, but she got along well all through her school career because of her social adaptability. She was not so averse to camping as her stepsister but she preferred tennis, dances, shows, and cards. She did not have initiative enough to obtain a job and had never been able to save from her allowance, so that she frequently borrowed from other members of the family. She had wealthier friends than the Haywood children and, though this was a source of pride to her, it sometimes caused dissatisfaction with her lot because she could not keep up with her friends in expenditures. She got along with the rest of the family fairly well; the only times animosities were aroused were when her shirking laid extra burdens on the others.

Peter Jones, 17, was well built, good looking, with a ready smile and a pleasant personality. Happy and care-free, more or less of a genius at fixing things around the house, he still managed to be absent when irksome duties like shovelling snow or hauling ashes were to be performed. "Bull-headed when he had once formed an opinion or desire, he would never fight or argue about whether others liked his ideas or not, but would go right on with his plans and carry them out contrary to others' wishes, pleas, or orders." He was "a lover of the outdoors, especially fond of tramping the woods with a rifle on his arm and 'pinking' at extraordinary targets; always ready for any sport, be it baseball, swimming, tennis, football, or ping-pong." He had no great ambition and never looked conscientiously for a summer job. He was thrifty with his allowance, however, and was always saving up for a new gun or other coveted possession. His school work was mediocre because of lack of effort. His ready smile and likable manner made him many friends. His stepbrother and he had many friends in common. His family contacts were usually smooth and happy, but sometimes his stubbornness aroused the wrath of others. He was his mother's pet and could tease and wheedle her into seeing his point of view.

The father was the real leader of the family. Mrs. Haywood's attempts at directing the family were never very successful, for they vacillated between domination and looseness of authority. The antagonisms between her and Robert were kept hidden for the most part from the rest of the family so that the others did not need to take sides. Among the children Robert was generally the leader. The only noticeable clique was between Mrs. Haywood and her own son, Peter. The regular home duties were well allocated. Besides looking after their rooms and doing odd work around the house, the children did the dinner dishes, the boys one night and the girls the next. "All in all our family group carried on in quite a businesslike manner, and although the boys rebelled a great deal over the ignominy of doing dishes, the duties were quite well distributed and carried out."

The summer was the only time that the family had many activities in common. The children were away from home a great deal during the winter, engaged in their clubs, social functions or recreations. Sometimes two or more of the children would be together, but often not. The parents went together to shows or stayed at home to read. "The sense of 'we' never stood out clearly in our family's minds unless we were being held up to the scrutiny of some outsider." There was no family custom or ritual. The principal aim of both parents was to give the children opportunities for development, especially education.

The father's income has dropped to approximately $3500 but this has brought no fundamental alteration in the pattern of family member positions.

The principal changes in Mr. Haywood are that he is much more nervous than before the decrease and therefore occasionally "flies off the handle," and that he is more of a family man than ever. He has made his recreational expense smaller by cutting out golf and long fishing trips, and insists that other members make similar curtailments. He is still a believer in education and is keeping the children in college at great sacrifices.

The depression has "done wonders for" Mrs. Haywood, "taking her mind from herself and making her think of others to a greater extent. Her 'ills' have nearly disappeared now that her mind is taken up with problems of stretching her kitchen dollar further than ever and keeping the home up-to-date and clean without new furnishings and the help of a cleaning woman. She spends more of her time with her husband now and seems to be much closer to him and understanding of him than before. She also seems to have forgotten her jealous feeling for Robert and now greets him heartily when he comes home and makes as much over him as she does over any of the rest, even catering at times to his personal taste in cooking foods. Her attitude toward the children has become more affectionate and she does herself proud in making them all happy and comfortable under existing conditions."

Robert has been sobered by the decrease and is now earnestly making the most of his opportunities. He saved enough from his job in Detroit to enter the University Engineering School and is working for his board and room. He has devoted himself to his studies and has received good grades. His friends are a few boys like himself who are seriously interested in their college work but like to enjoy themselves occasionally too. His feeling for his father and sister are just the same, but he has more affection for the step-relatives.

Jane is attending junior college at home and has helped by clerking in the summer. She is much the same and liked by every one.

Mary is the only one whom the decrease has not

changed for the better. She is as healthy and lazy and inefficient as ever and now is annoyed because she cannot have as many good times as before. She graduated from a two-year normal course, held down a job for a semester and then gave it up because the little town was too confining for one of her tastes. She even contracted debts that her salary could not take care of and thus was an added burden to her stepfather. Though her laziness at home comes in for pointed remarks, she seems oblivious and remains fairly cheerful. Her frequent dates are her main interest in life.

Peter is also at junior college. He has gone through much the same change as his stepbrother and takes things more seriously than before. His academic work is better. He has saved his allowance for clothes instead of spending it on guns. He has got out from under his mother's wing and stands on his own feet.

The decrease has meant of course that the family's material equipment in the way of house furnishings, sporting equipment, the car, and even clothes are not as up-to-date as before.

The family situation has become more democratic. The father is still the leader, but, because the children are more serious, there can be more participation by them in family decisions. The only clique that existed before, that between Mrs. Haywood and her own son, has now disappeared.

There is much more common life in the home due perhaps at the expense of outside amusements. "Each thinks now more of the others' feelings and wishes than before."

———

The double step-parent, stepchild relationship in Case No. 13 is an obvious reason for regarding the family originally as only moderately integrated. There is more question concerning the correctness of the highly adaptable classification. This was adopted in view of the business-like leadership of Mr. Haywood and the apparent willingness of his wife and the children to conform to the pattern of family life which he regarded as wise and efficient. Despite the rather selfish behavior of Mary since the change, the family seems to be maintaining or even bettering its integration and must therefore be regarded as having been firmly invulnerable to a similar-positions decrease.

The six other cases illustrating the same type situation are interesting variants of No. 13. Case No. 51 is the wholesale lumberman's family that we met in Chapter II. It will be remembered that the father's crudities were the chief cause of family friction. Case No. 30 describes an orthodox Jewish family in which the son had rebelled somewhat from the parental ways and in which there was not a great deal of common activity. In No. 35 the household group consisted of the parents, one child and the paternal grandmother. The wife and her mother-in-law did not get along very well, but the situation improved after the decrease in income. Case No. 42 is very nearly a Type I family, but there was not quite the community of interests which is characteristic of that type. The four children went their separate ways and there was little family activity as a unit. In No. 15 the wife was a stepmother to the two children and they looked upon her more as a housekeeper than a mother. With the onset of the decrease the group was brought more together and the sense of solidarity increased. Case No. 24 concerns a farming family where there was no great enthusiasm for family contacts and affairs, though all were amicable. The reaction of the decrease upon the father in this case will be subject for further comment in Chapter XII. There we will also meet No. 13, No. 15, No. 30, and No. 35 again.

These Type IV cases show a uniformly greater awareness of their solidarity under the pressure of a similar-positions decrease, an improvement in awareness which is even more marked than that noted for Type I cases. The reason perhaps is that there is more room for improvement here; highly integrated families can call out few unifying energies not already being used, while moderately integrated families, if highly adaptable, are likely, in meeting the challenge, to become much more aware of their unity than before.

Let us turn now to our one example of a Type

IV case undergoing a decrease with modified positions.

CASE NO. 52

The Bulkleys are a family of five consisting of the father, who, at the time of the decrease, was 44, mother 45, girls of 17 and 16, and a boy of 14. They lived in Royal Oak, Michigan, one of the satellite towns adjacent to Detroit. Being a rather prominent family in this community, they dwelt in one of the better residential sections. Their house was a roomy, eight-room structure with a landscaped yard, and the family possessed two cars, a piano, radio, a boat with outboard motor and a camping outfit. Mr. Bulkley owned and operated a small mill. His yearly income was approximately $6500.

Mr. Bulkley was a conscientious, optimistic, kindly man who devoted practically all his time to his business. Perhaps his chief fault was occasional stubbornness. "He enjoyed his work, but could cast aside all business cares to go on a hunting or fishing trip. During the early part of his married life he had spent practically all his leisure time in his home, but as business increased and he could afford to devote more time to outside interests without depriving his family, he joined the Masonic Lodge, Elks, the Rotary Club, a country club and various sport clubs in Northern Michigan. Naturally his acquaintanceship was wide and varied. He was interested in politics and had little

129

interest in purely social activities, but his wife enjoyed them and he went out to most of the functions.

"Physically a large man, possessing candid eyes, a deep voice and a hearty laugh, he kept himself immaculate in good tailor-made clothing. A slight limp (caused by a serious fall) embarrassed him slightly. He had no objection to smoking and drinking—done in moderation and in the proper place by the proper persons." He seldom attended church "but insisted that the children go, for he believed that a certain amount of religious training was necessary for every one. His most intimate friends were those who enjoyed hunting and fishing and who were fairly well educated." He was willing to work long and hard to give his family the best of everything. He was liberal also, in giving to charity. His family relations were good, though he did not spend much time with his children. He did not like to be bothered with family disputes. His favorite was his son.

Mrs. Bulkley was "alert, extremely energetic, gentle but sometimes impatient" and took life more seriously than did her husband. She was wrapped up in her children but also liked helping the less fortunate in the community. "She could enjoy the luxuries of life and still be contented to prepare a dinner for the family. The greater proportion of her outside activities was connected with church work. A garden club, Women's League of Nations and other civic organizations were of interest to her. For friends she chose refined and intellectual women many of whom were parents of her children's friends. Having no private income she was scrupulous with the household money. She did all of the girls' sewing as well as a great deal of her own. Too, she found time to do her own housework, with the help of a woman one day a week." She showed no favoritism among the children. She had her way in regard to the family's social life, but her husband was the final authority in all money matters.

Carol,* the elder girl, was a senior in high school, an honor student, member of a journalistic society, and interested in reading and stamps. She liked basketball and baseball, enjoyed going to Detroit for concerts, and was a frequent attendant at the movies. She was care-free, not overly energetic, sometimes rather unpleasant to her family and others. She had inferiority feelings which she covered by being very outspoken. When she had some supervision, she would work with a will, because the supervision gave her confidence. When she was on her own, she was likely to be half-hearted. She had earned little money and spent her allowance rather foolishly. Her acquaintance had been growing through high school and her inferiority feelings diminishing. She pitied her younger sister who seemed to her still a child. She liked her mother and father equally well, but confided in her mother almost exclusively.

Ruth, the younger girl, was fiery, red-haired, and extreme in her reactions. If she was interested in something, she would pursue it enthusiastically; if not, she would have nothing to do with it. "Her chief interests were athletics, art, and music. She was constantly being entertained or entertaining. She was not self-conscious and therefore happy most of the time. She belonged to the various high-school clubs and other social clubs. For her friends she chose lively, ambitious youngsters of good families. The majority of her friends were younger than she, probably because she had never quite grown up. Occasionally she earned a little money, like her sister, by staying evenings with children of friends of her parents. She and her sister had frequent intervals of antagonism, and Ruth was often driven to tears by Carol's assumptions of superiority and greater worldly wisdom. But on the whole they were good friends."

James possessed a sort of dual personality. "To outsiders he appeared to be a quiet, intelligent boy, perhaps a trifle proud. To those who knew him better he was very witty. To his family he was often a sullen, impudent boy, but when he chose to be nice he was so charming one forgot his sulkiness. He assumed a superior attitude, correcting every statement about which there might be chance of error and one seldom found him wrong. He was very alert and had excellent scholastic grades. He was just old enough to begin playing basketball and he put all his energy into it. He was very perseverant and would not leave anything undone. He was active in scout work and attended summer camps, bringing home many badges. He got his greatest enjoyment from reading worthwhile books and magazines, especially pertaining to natural history, some of which might seem beyond his comprehension. He peddled papers and earned quite a bit, much of which was saved." He had bought his own bicycle and scout uniform this way. He had plenty of friends, many of whom were from families like his own, but some of whom were not approved by the parents. However, he would not give them up.

The children had been given music, dancing and elocution lessons and had been in summer camps two or three years each. Mr. and Mrs. Bulkley wanted them to have every opportunity.

There was friendly rivalry among the children for school grades, athletic success and social status. At times there were bitter quarrels. Mr. Bulkley had never had anything to do with household duties, other than giving Mrs. Bulkley the biweekly check. The girls did the evening dishes and in the summer saw to watering the lawn.

The family solidarity was not as great as it might have been. Many of Mr. Bulkley's friends were not acquainted with Mrs. Bulkley and *vice versa.* The former's business kept him away from home a great deal. He never attended church, while the mother and children did. She disapproved the little drinking that her husband did. "I can't recall any common activities we all participated in except the regular Sunday afternoon drive, which became more or less a bore to all of us. During the summer, though, we did enjoy family picnics. It was a family custom that every one must be home to observe all birthdays and the wedding anniversary. Holidays were always observed with either the mother's or the father's family." The family members tried to help one another when in trouble. The children tended to be a bit jealous of each other's successes, however, and the fortunate one was likely to be a little overbearing. On the whole discipline was sympathetic but strict. There was a good deal of pride in the minds of all members because of the standing of the family in the community.

The decrease affected this family in a complicated way. The father's business was dependent on new building and when that began to fall off in 1930 the income shrank. By 1931 it was recognized that the situation was not a temporary one, and the home was mortgaged to pay the business creditors. The mill was shut down for lack of orders. That fall, in order not to disappoint Carol's expectations of attending the University, the home was rented and the family moved to Ann Arbor. Mr. Bulkley, after fruitless attempts to get work for his mill, early in 1932 secured a job with the service department of a large automobile concern. Because he thought that former employees of his who were higher up in the same organization pitied him, he asked to be transferred to the factory. Here, however, the work was too strenuous for him and he finally had to give it up. He was without work for the last half of 1932 and the first quarter of 1933. Then he got a contract to build a small home which helped the family enormously in paying up debts. But he still has no permanent work.

Mr. Bulkley has changed considerably due to the strain. He is not so cheerful as formerly, but he is even more energetic, and is determined not to let the depression get the best of him. Because he has not been able to afford medical attention, his hip is worse and he is becoming more lame. He is very sensitive over the decline of his fortunes. He has had to drop all his clubs and his only recreation is in taking the boat and going fishing on an occasional Sunday. His friends have proved to be true ones, for they continue to keep in touch with him and give him all the assistance they can. It does him good to be with them, for he regains some of his self-esteem. He has nothing but sympathy for the rest of the family and would do anything possible for them.

Mrs. Bulkley has as much energy as ever but she has become a little embittered and sometimes says things which hurt her husband. "Yet her love for him has deepened and she almost hates any one who does anything contrary to his plans." She has not many friends in Ann Arbor, and this gives her too much opportunity to brood over the family misfortunes. Although she struggles against it, she is becoming less tolerant. She misses her church connections most. When she has time she reads light fiction because it takes her mind off her troubles. She also listens to the radio a great deal for recreation. Always economical, she has become very frugal—to the extent of shutting off the electric ice box in the winter and using the fruit cellar instead.

At first it was difficult for Carol to adjust herself to the change. She did not appreciate the sacrifices her family were making to give her a university education, and she did not devote herself to her academic work as consistently as she should have. She was a little bitter about the joke life was playing on her family, but is now happier, having come to realize that other families are even "worse off." She has only three friends in the community and, since she belongs to no organization on the campus, feels rather out of things. She appreciates her family now more than ever before.

Ruth is also now in the University, a physical education major. She has matured, controls her feelings better than before and maintains a fairly optimistic outlook, despite the family troubles. She expects to begin making a little money soon, refereeing school games. The majority of her friends are girls in her department. She does not "date" much but seems to enjoy vicariously the good times of her friends.

James is now a rather sophisticated high-school senior who tries to hide his feelings, but who is nevertheless rather bitter about the situation. To cover up his true sentiments, he adopts a loud, bois-terous manner which is very annoying to the rest of the family. His friends have much better clothes and more spending money than he, which is of course hard to bear. He is interested in scout work and is captain of one of the athletic teams, a class officer, in dramatic work and a member of the glee club. He manages to go to many parties and thus has a good time in spite of his lack of pocket money.

The family is fortunate in having a nice house on the outskirts of town with a lawn and yard which they can be proud of. The old cars are still in service, but the family goes without telephone and other things which formerly seemed to be necessities.

The Bulkleys are a more united family than before. After readjusting to the extent required for the greater degree of co-operation necessary, the members "came to know and understand each other much better. The luncheon and the dinner table have become the center for the exchange of the day's happenings, where formerly dining was a process of hurrying and getting through with the dishes. We all respect this custom in deference to mother, whose day is long and lonely. Mother and Dad spend the evening reading or talking and the rest of us study."

The mother is perhaps a little more of a family leader now than the father. She keeps the family morale up more than any other one, though all the children feel so sorry for the father that they too help in this. The family duties are fairly allocated and consistently carried out, the girls helping their mother and James looking after the yard and the carrying out of ashes.

None of the family goes to church now, largely because there is no money for the collection plate. The whole family, however, often listens to a radio church service.

The degree of co-operation is greatly increased. The girls type their father's letters and specifications for him, Mrs. Bulkley takes over the girls' tasks when they are pressed by their studies, and so on. The children are still proud of their parents and think their family is a superior one.

———

This is a case where there might be differences of interpretation in at least two directions. Some might question the characterization of high adaptability.[1] My defense would be that the members, save only Carol, were careful with money, and were not attached to material values, and that the household was run very carefully and systematically, with discussion by the parents of pecuniary matters. The modified positions characterization might also raise doubts. Mr. Bulkley remained the only breadwinner, but his change of status was so great and the others had to pitch in and help in so many ways to which they had not been accustomed before that the situation seemed to be beyond the limits of a similar-positions decrease. The change in place of residence is another circumstance which deserves consideration, but that will be discussed in Chapter XII.

The shifts in roles corresponding to the shifts in positions have been made effectively in this instance and it therefore seems eminently proper to regard the results as showing that Type IV families are readjustively invulnerable to a decrease with modified positions. The heightened sense of integration is again an evocation of unsuspected potentialities.

Case No. 34 is our only family of this type encountering a decrease with changed positions.

CASE NO. 34

The Pikes were, at the time of the decrease, of

[1] Mr. Fuller, who assisted me by classifying the cases independently, felt "mediocre adaptability" more accurate.

the following ages: father 51, mother 45, John 22, Florence 19, Martha* 18. They lived in Ann Arbor where Mr. Pike was an engineer. He had an income of approximately $4400 a year. Since their marriage Mr. and Mrs. Pike had made their home in several cities in the Middle West, moving as Mr. Pike found better opportunities to practice his profession. At this time they lived in a modern nine-room stucco house situated in a nice residential district, with front and back yard filled with shrubbery and trees.

Mr. Pike's affairs took him away from home a great deal so that he was not close to his children. He took care of all money matters and tended to be a little high-handed with reference to them. He was strict with the children and they felt sometimes that he did not understand them. His principal recreations were watching athletic events and playing golf. He was a member of a golf club and of the Masonic order. His friends were engineers and other professional men of his own type. He was capable, sincere, loyal.

Mrs. Pike was chiefly interested in young people, both her own children and the others in the community. Just before moving to Ann Arbor she had been president of a Parent-Teachers Association and county chairman of the Children's Welfare League. Her club activities were her chief recreation. She taught in Sunday School and was active in an organization interested in developing musical talent among colored people. Since coming to Ann Arbor she had taken English courses in the University. Her friends were women of her general type. To her family she was always attentive and just, though her marked nervousness sometimes made relations a little difficult.

John was the healthiest and most energetic individual in the family. He was a university senior, specializing in geology. He participated in sports of all kinds and was athletic director of his college fraternity. On the whole he had a wholesome outlook on life, was good-natured and kindly, though occasionally forgetful of little things about the house, a trait which annoyed his mother. He tended to be rather careless of his personal appearance also. Once in a while he would drink and play poker with his college chums—another sore point with his mother. He was an officer in the Young People's League at his church. He had worked in the summers with a construction company. His only jealousy of other family members was provoked by the relatively greater expenditure of the family's funds for the girls' clothes than for his.

Florence, though physically robust, had little energy. She was a student at the University taking a combined literary-nursing course. Her chief activities were reading and dancing. She was constantly trying to keep her weight down and was thus impairing her health somewhat. Her mother

141

and she were rather antagonistic on this subject, the former feeling her efforts were silly and harmful. Her friends were the ordinary type at the University. Occasionally she would be jealous of her sister, and on the whole she had more difficulties in her family relations than did any other member.

Martha was a strong, energetic friendly sort. At this time she was a university freshman and found herself enjoying it very much. Like her brother she was athletic, playing both golf and tennis and liking to swim. She was also interested in poetry and teaching Sunday School. The latter activity enabled her to indulge her love of children. She was a leader in Girl Scouts and Campfire work. The only members of the family whom she rubbed the wrong way at all were her father and sister, who were occasionally annoyed by her flippancy and expenditures for clothes respectively.

The family was rather loosely organized. Each one had his own interests and pursued them. There was little family custom, little sharing of joys and sorrows, the main tie being a common interest in doing worth-while things. Each had his field of interest and the others were glad of the achievements of each, but at the same time there was not a little rivalry and jealousy. When the family was attacked from outside the solidarity would definitely increase for the time being. The children did no chores to speak of around the home. It must be said, however, that the children held the hope some day of repaying what their parents had done for them by enabling them to retire without financial worries. This was a vague ideal and was not immediately motivating, for none of them saved anything.

The decrease was at first merely that, but after about a year the father's income stopped almost entirely because of the absence of new construction. The family rented its house and moved into a three-room apartment. The other members began looking for work. Mrs. Pike and Martha located jobs very quickly. John located a board-and-room job and no longer lived with the rest. Mr. Pike has had odd jobs as a day laborer. The family is living on $600 a year. Food costs $7 a week and the rent is $28 a month. There are almost no other expenditures.

Mr. Pike has managed to keep up his morale remarkably in the face of disaster and a complete change in his position as the family's sole support. His occasional jobs as a laborer take up very little of his time. The balance he spends helping at home and doing professional reading. He is much closer to his children than before.

The mother has proven her mettle also. She has taken work—washing, ironing, house-cleaning and taking care of children. What little leisure she has she spends keeping up her studies. She has found out that her best friends of the past were rather selfish and not helpful to her in this time of need. She has made new friends of a less intellectual but more substantial sort.

Florence and her father, being the only ones without outside jobs, do the housework. John is attending the University part time, as well as working both for room and board and doing odd jobs. He feels the depression the most because of his shabby clothes. The girls are not in such a bad situation because they can make their clothes over.

The children have realized that it is up to them to help the family through its difficulties and have all pitched in with a will. They still find opportunity for much recreation in and around Ann Arbor. Because of necessity they share each other's possessions, and their petty jealousies have vanished.

The parents withdraw to their bedroom whenever the girls want to entertain at home and otherwise all try to smooth out the difficult situations. The family really seems to be happier, at least as far as its internal relations go, than before. They go around together much more and find delight in each other's companionship.

"We are living in a much saner, healthier and finer attitude than ever before. When my father does resume work again he will be far more capable because he has at last a family which is an understanding one and we will never again **fail** each other as we have in the past."

————

This case is in many respects comparable with No. 4, the family which proved itself invulnerable by readjusting successfully when the father served a prison sentence. They are the only two illustrations in our series of high adaptability meeting such a severe pressure. And the result in both cases is family heroism of a high order. The Pikes have done a quite remarkable job of rearranging their family roles to suit their new positions. It is indeed rare that so marked shifts can be accomplished with so little hard feeling and friction.

Our conclusions regarding Type IV are very similar to those we arrived at for Type I. Since there was not in these families the same degree of solidarity to begin with, and since there was at least an equal likelihood that the potential solidarity was not being manifested actually, the results show even more change for the better than was true with the Type I families. The weaknesses in original integration took various forms, some of which were the divergence of children's standards from those of their parents, rivalry among the children, favoritisms of one or both parents for particular children, and generally individualistic organization. However, none of these was severe enough with this type family to produce the lack of family structure which we will see in Types VII and VIII. There is enough backbone here to serve as a basis for adaptability. However, given sufficient structure, it is clearly demonstrated that high adaptability is more important for meeting a decrease than high integration.

CHAPTER VIII

MODERATELY INTEGRATED, MODERATELY ADAPTABLE FAMILIES

TYPE V cases are more plentiful in our series than those of any other type. Since moderate integration and moderate adaptability occupy median positions in our scale of qualities, this is not surprising. Of the 14 families classified here, nine suffered a simple decrease; three, one with modified positions; and two, one with changed positions. From what we have seen of the similarity between Types I and IV we might expect that Type V would prove very like Type II. Certainly it resembles more closely Type II, from which it differs only by one degree of integration, than it does Type IV, from which it differs by one degree of adaptability.

Our illustration of the similar-positions decrease for Type V is Case No. 37.

CASE NO. 37

The Lehmann family was composed at the time of the decrease of the father 53, the mother 52, and two children, Karl 23, and Charlotte* 20. They lived in a large brick house on a half acre plot in one of the North Shore residential suburbs of Chicago. The interior furnishings were elaborate and the garden was beautifully landscaped. Other wealthy families lived in the neighborhood. There were two cars, a Cadillac and a Hudson.

Mr. Lehmann was of German-Jewish descent. He had been a professor of English when a younger man and had earned the doctorate of philosophy. When he had found how small his income was to be, he had decided to go into advertising. He also became the local representative of a national chair company, and had made a marked success of it. Later he purchased a small household equipment business which he ran himself with the expectation that his son would some day take it over. In good years before the depression his income from his three businesses and from his investments amounted to $40,000.

Mr. Lehmann "was extremely even-tempered and patient but when finally aroused, very severe. Being very intelligent and socially-minded, he weighed his actions very carefully, never acting upon impulse or anger. His philosophy of life was sincere and broad; it was that people do what they do because they are what they are. But he didn't let it go at that—he tried to help, encourage, or correct; but when aroused he dominated, unless the individual attempted to rationalize with him. Although he possessed the power of sympathetic insight he was not at all scientific, and hence irrational at times. He was a man who thought things out for himself, usually sanely and correctly."

He took several extended vacations each year to Florida, or up in Canada, fishing. His other amusements included swimming and playing bridge. The latter he played seriously and carefully. He also did a great deal of serious reading. He had once taken up golf but quit it when he found it made him nervously tired. His clubs included the Exchange Club and a yacht club where he swam and played bridge. One of his sidelines was the editing of a local civic sheet which he had started in order to fight the political corruption in his community. He had thus been successful in instigating many reforms.

Mr. Lehmann's friends were both Jews and Gentiles but his most intimate ones were Gentiles. They were intelligent and prosperous men—any one who did not answer these requirements was not interesting to him. "He cared a great deal whether a person commanded a rather high position in the world. In various quasi-business participations such as the Better Business Bureau and the Community Fund he knew well many prominent men of Chicago, so that he had a great deal of influence in several fields."

He never drank nor smoked, and his only gambling was to play bridge for low stakes. He mingled easily with intelligent companions and had a very keen, subtle sense of humor. With all this he was essentially an introvert and did not tell any one much of what he was thinking.

Mr. Lehmann's relations with his wife at this time were rather distant. They found that they quarrelled a good deal and so went their separate ways with as little friction as possible. His attitude toward his son, who had always been a problem child because of mental abnormalities, was one of deep concern, though his patience and kindliness had been worn thin by repeated disillusionments. This situation was complicated by Mrs. Lehmann who often thought he was dealing too harshly with the boy and would secretly give him privileges. All of his devotion, much of which would normally have been given to his wife and son, was therefore lavished on his daughter, Charlotte. "Although he did not lavish money on her as he did affection, he did satisfy her every wish in a modest way. He told her just prior to the decrease not to worry about money, that he was able to give her anything she needed and wanted."

Mrs. Lehmann had not been well for long periods and, though at this time quite healthy, she was still impatient and irritable when tired. She was intelligent but at the same time unreasonable. She was honest, sincere and loyal, but a prey to her emotions. She scorned all superficialities and reduced life to simple formulas based upon her early Catholic rearing.

She was very fond of all sorts of social activities and was an ardent swimmer (which she had learned to do when middle-aged), loved the movies, and played a great deal of bridge. She had always hated housework, and, now that her children were grown up, she did not have to bother with it. She was away from home from breakfast until dinner at night. Her allowance was very liberal but it was never spent extravagantly. She kept a budget and saved almost as much as she spent.

Though she admired her husband greatly, she could not refrain from criticizing him. There was jealousy of his sisters, of whom he was very fond and whom he helped financially. She loved her son blindly and in spite of his misdemeanors, and protected him as much as she could. Toward her daughter she was very nice but not particularly affectionate. They were very different types and just "got along."

Karl was a tall, wiry person of 23 with a childish face. He was a very peculiar type and psychiatrists had been unable to diagnose his difficulty or help him much. He was not affectionate, and yet he was very sensitive to his family's disapproval. He was intellectually brilliant, but untruthful and highly imaginative. He would risk anything in order to appear as a wealthy, reckless dare-devil—money, cars, even his life. He wrote excellent poetry but did not persevere. "He had no occupation. He attended a university until he got tired of it, and played bridge at such high stakes that he needed money desperately. He even got into trouble with the police. He did not have many physical recreations nor did he pursue very strenuously at this time his hobby for stamp-collecting. He seemed to be in a state of mental lethargy except that he was in love with a fairly wealthy girl who was nearly a genius and considered herself to be one. She was an important factor in his needing money; she was used to having a lot and was a demanding person. He lavished money on her in all sorts of foolish ways."

Despite his shortcomings Karl always managed to have nice friends. They were above the average in intelligence and of accepted social position.

Karl had little use for his father. Toward his mother he showed indifference and anger, for he wished she would leave him alone and stop trying to impose her hopes upon him. His sister "was the only one for whom he ever let on that he cared. He would often seek out her company in spite of the fact that she never understood him."

Charlotte was a tall, thin, agreeable, sensitive girl. She was a normal sort who took a great deal of enjoyment in going to dances, parties, having nice clothes and so on. She was engaged to a very worth-while young man and enjoying it thoroughly. She was intelligent but not very deep or philosophically minded. Her attention was divided between getting good grades at the University and having a good time. Dancing, swimming, horseback riding and a little tennis provided her with exercise.

She was naturally thrifty and saved money from her allowance even though she did not need to. She had a small circle of girl friends who were a motley lot—a florist's daughter, the police chief's daughter, a society girl, etc. Her fiancé was the most superior of her associates. He was very alert mentally though difficult to get along with because of his temper and self-centeredness.

She was very fond of her father, tried to be pleasant to her mother, and was as friendly as possible with her brother.

The family considered itself definitely an intellectual one. Mr. Lehmann especially played an important part here. He encouraged a high scholastic record and good reading in the children and never allowed a cheap magazine in the house.

The most powerful clique in the family was that between the father and daughter. The children had few home duties. Karl helped his mother more than Charlotte did, for she always contrived to find something to do with her father. The children were very independent and unwilling to go on drives or to the movies with their parents. "They wished to participate in their own activities. There was no family custom or ritual except that the members must arrive at meals on time. Each member was an entity in himself except as far as money and perhaps a stray feeling of security now and then was needed. The joys and sorrows were not known to the whole group, much less shared. The members helped each other when the occasion arose but there was no aim toward which all four members were striving.

"The members had a proud sense of 'we' because they were proud of each other and themselves. Each member saw in the other a unique individual, intelligent above all *and* a member of the family. There always had been a strong family feeling in spite of verbal convictions to the contrary expressed by the younger members in time of stress."

The decrease came gradually but drastically to this family until Mr. Lehmann's $40,000 income was down, in 2 years, to $3,000. The chair company which he represented locally went into bankruptcy, so that he now has just two sources of revenue, neither of which is bringing in much.

The decrease has made him physically weaker, and narrower in his outlook. He suffered a nervous breakdown when the heaviest blow struck and is now not so alert as formerly. He is quieter, hardly ever humorous, but never complains and cannot endure others doing so. "He has turned from thoughts of material possession to spiritual ones. He sits thinking now for long periods." Recreations have remained about the same except that there are no expensive trips. He has retained his club memberships. He has withdrawn from all active community work. He tries to read a great deal, but is so nervously exhausted that he falls asleep in the chair.

He is very frugal now, buying, for instance, ready-made suits in place of very expensive tailor-made ones which he used to purchase. His friends remain about the same, but he does not say so much about their wealth as formerly.

He gives in to his wife much more. "He has lost his spunk." She runs the house and he waits on her. "The depression has brought them together; they have time to get acquainted with each other again. His attitude toward his son is one of resignation. He still helps him financially but has given up expecting much of him. He still loves his daughter, but has to hide it from his wife who is displeased at her daughter's marriage. He is very fond of the granddaughter who has come to live with the grandparents. He is careful not to spoil her, while doing everything he can for her.

Mrs. Lehmann "has lost the will to live. She is very bitter about the present conditions and especially about her extreme ill health. She has a chronic asthma which has not yielded to operators and the care of specialists. She considers herself a handicap to every one. She goes out very little because her health does not permit any windy or night air, excitement or fatigue. The worst shock was that she can never swim again.

"Her allowance is about one-fourth of what it was and she has a hard time making ends meet.

She has very few clothes. Many of her friends have dropped away because she was unable to join them in their parties. However, her most intimate friends are constant."

Her family attitudes are better. She appreciates her husband's real worth more than she did and she is less intense and therefore less wearing on him. She is less fiercely maternal toward her son but still affectionate and kind. Toward Charlotte there is little change. Charlotte's baby "is the light in her life. She adores her. She is very kind to her and is a good influence except when she gets tired. Then she loses patience with the child."

Karl has been married since the decrease and this has helped his adjustment considerably. He wants to work but cannot find a job. He has a much saner view of his responsibilities in life. He earns enough to pay his apartment rent each week by working in the parents' yard and around the house. He still spends what little additional money he gets recklessly, sometimes going hungry as a result. He is more submissive toward his father because of his financial dependence, and more independent of his mother. He is openly jealous of his sister and her child and is afraid that they will get more than their share of the family care and money.

Charlotte married about the time of the decrease and continued in her university work. When the baby came it seemed better to keep her at the parents' home because Charlotte had a self-supporting job which was helping both her husband and herself through school. She is little changed except that she is more mature. Not living at home, she is not so close to her father, but otherwise her family relations are unchanged.

The family no longer thinks of itself as intellectual or successful. The members have lost considerable of their morale. The pride is still in the background, however. The neighbors do not hold aloof as before; "they feel a new easy manner in the broken spirit."

Mrs. Lehmann is given more leadership. This is conceded by the others more to keep peace than it is deserved by her merits. Confined to her home and its narrow sphere now, she becomes very emotional about little things and the others would rather let her make the decisions than create difficult situations. This is no doubt due in part to sympathy because of her health.

There is rivalry within the family group as before. But it is fairer. "This is one result of the depression. No one wants to hit a man when he's down and when you're down yourself you would like to help other members to get where you are even though it may be only a little higher.

"There is an indescribable, indefinable drawing together, a uniting of sympathetic forces against adversity. Each member's welfare means something to the other members. Joys and sorrows are shared by all because of this new bond of sympathy."

————

Although the Lehmanns had the highest income of any Type V family, their adjustment is typical of the others experiencing a similar-positions decrease. Family cliques made them only moderately integrated to begin with and the way in which they took a high standard of living for granted detracted from their adaptability. The marriage of the two children was a unique factor in the case but it did not markedly change the family positions. The subsequent adjustment shows that they were capable of enduring this sort of decrease, and it even seemed to bring them a little closer.

The nine cases in the same situation as No. 37 have the highest average original income ($11,-200) of any group in our series. Perhaps this is because wealthy families are likely to become accustomed to a way of life in which material values play a prominent role, so that their adaptability is affected. Also their common life is not so much of a struggle, so that integration is perhaps less often very strong.

The occupations of the fathers in the other families were: dentist, banker, real-estate agent (2), corporation official, accountant, travelling salesman, and skilled mechanic. Four of the cases showed definite friction between parents and children or among the children, while the remaining four were simply instances of loose family organization, with few common activities or interests. The reasons for their moderate degree of adaptability were more various. In two, No. 12 and No. 18, the father was easy-going and rather irresponsible; two others, No. 16 and No. 39, had notions of the aristocratic character of the family, while three more, No. 3, No. 7 and No. 38, were wedded to a high standard of living. In the last case, No. 21, it is difficult to place one's finger on any one characteristic tending toward unadaptability, unless it be the irresponsibility of the son, yet one feels that the family had a certain rigidity which was a handicap when the need for adjustment came.

The only one of the nine cases in which there was any alteration in positions at all was No. 21, which was used in Chapter III as the example of the extreme similar-positions situation. The cases all came through the experience of the decrease with their integration intact, though in one or two there was not a little wavering and uncertainty for a while. In this respect Type V families seem to be slightly inferior to Type II ones. This suggests that integration is a variable of some significance, at least for meeting a simple decrease. Four of these, No. 3, No. 16, No. 18, and No. 39, will be discussed again in Chapter XII.

We may now turn to the three Type V cases

which were subjected to the stronger pressure of modified positions. Our example will be No. 10.

CASE NO. 10

The Burton family was comprised of the father and mother and four children, Lester* 19, Harry 17, Frances 14, and Elizabeth 11. Mr. Burton was a wholesale merchant and they lived in the nicest residential section of Saginaw, Michigan. They owned a completely equipped 13-room wooden house situated on a 75- by 100-foot lot which contained a three-car garage, a rock garden, and a fine lawn shaded by apple trees. The neighbors were leading business and professional men. The family owned two medium-priced cars. Mr. Burton's income was about $10,000 a year.

Mr. Burton was a man of even temperament, patient, kind, happy, and contented. He was very energetic and willing to tackle anything. "He continually had a smile on his face and a sympathetic ear for all who were not as fortunate as he. He seemed to take life as a great adventure and faced it with a light heart." He was a "good citizen" and accepted and practised the conventional moral code. He was a member of the Board of Directors of the local Y.M.C.A. and he also belonged to the Knights Templar. He was an active churchman. Throughout the city he was known as an able and honest business man. His friends were business men of the same type. His chief recreations were fishing and hunting. He was a model father, kind, without favoritism, and generous.

Mrs. Burton was a tall, thin woman who enjoyed good health. She was vivacious, ambitious and young in spirit. Both of her parents had been born in England and she was perhaps a little English in her stubbornness. Her main interest in life was her children and she was kind and thoughtful toward them. Her outside activities were largely determined by her husband's interests. She took an active part in the Ladies Auxiliary of the Knights Templar, in the church, and in a married people's dancing club which both she and her husband enjoyed. Her friends were almost entirely the wives of her husband's business friends.

"She liked the home work and did her own cooking and cleaning and taking care of us children, although my father was desirious of a servant. The only work about the house sent out was the washing." She was very similar to her husband in general outlook—conservative and highly moral in the conventional pattern. Both she and her husband were total abstainers from alcohol. She showed a little favoritism in her family relations toward the two youngest children.

The older boy, Lester, was late in maturing and he had been small for his age all through his youth. He was quiet and unassuming but if angered would carry a grudge for a long time. He suffered from acute inferiority feelings and was especially afraid of mingling with girls. He would go to no functions where he would have to associate with them. He was interested more in athletics, and despite his size, he had achieved some success in handball, swimming, and golf. He was a member of the Y.M.C.A. and most of his friends were boys he mingled with there. None of them smoked or drank or went out with girls. He did not associate at all with his younger brother's "swell" companions. Indeed he hated them.

He was ambitious and liked school. When the opportunity offered, he worked for his father in the shipping room, tallying and loading, or in the office, typing and filing. He had access to as much money as the other children but he did not spend it freely. He saved much both of his allowance and his earnings. He was a little domineering toward the other children, largely because he did not like their friends or their interests. He was also a little jealous of his mother's favoritism toward his brother. He was closest to his father and found his chief companionship within the family with him.

Harry was almost the antithesis of Lester. He was a large, easy-going boy. "He had no ambition whatsoever to do any work, either physical or mental. In school he was never brilliant and did not care for it, and instead of working outside for money, he was content with puttering around the house, doing odd jobs. His principal activities centered in a fraternity which he joined while in high school. He took an active interest in their dances and social functions, which were wide and varied. Hence he became associated with a social class which was quite in keeping with his father's income. He had a car any time he wanted, and was very lax and free with the money he was given." His associates were a bit "wild" and he learned both to smoke and to drink at an early age. He learned from them to be unambitious and wasteful with money. His friends had more to spend than he and he was therefore constantly trying to keep up with them. He was rather condescending toward the other members of the family, and he quarrelled with every one except his mother. He resented his brother's critical attitude toward his friends.

Frances, 14, was vivacious and energetic and took much interest in social life such as that represented by Harry's friends. She belonged to a sorority, the other members of which had money spent lavishly upon them by their wealthy parents. She had begun going out with boys a great deal. Her attitude toward the family was pleasant and was better than it had been some time before, when she had been childishly selfish. She fitted into the family group very well.

Elizabeth, because she was the youngest, had been babied considerably. She had little sense of responsibility and had everything she desired. "Although she was glad to have other children play with her toys, she did not hesitate to let the less fortunate ones know that they all belonged to her and that they were using them at her authorization, and that she could refuse further playing with them at her discretion. She was too young to realize where the money came from that bought all these toys, and took it simply as a matter of course, as if she were born to have them."

There was very little that the children did around the house in the way of chores. Lester was perfectly willing to work for money, but disliked odd jobs. Harry did a little, but most of these tasks were taken care of by two old men who were hired in the summer to cut the lawn and do other jobs around the house.

Personal relations in the family were strained— chiefly due to the antagonism between Lester and Harry. The father would side with Lester while the mother and Frances would take Harry's view. "There was a keen sense of rivalry between these two groups." The crux of the whole dispute was the conception of the family's social role—one group believing the family to be solid, middle class, and the other feeling that it was to be considered one of the wealthy, "society" families. However, the family would come to have a high degree of solidarity when outside opposition became evident. Even Lester and Harry would stand up for each other under these circumstances. There were also common celebrations on birthdays, Christmas, New Year's, and Thanksgiving. Often both paternal and maternal relatives would be present at these functions. The family rarely went out anywhere together. Each child felt co-operative toward the parents, but there was little inclination to be co-operative with each other.

The parents had tried to do everything possible for the development of their children. They had shown an interest in their school work, had bought them good books, and otherwise given them opportunities. Mrs. Burton's approval of Harry's associates would probably not have continued had she known that they drank. She quite naturally thought they must be good influences because they were from the "best" families in town.

Mr. Burton's business went from bad to worse, until finally he had to close it up entirely. The family decided to move to Ann Arbor so that Mr. Burton could take a sales job he had been offered, Mrs. Burton could help by taking in roomers, and the children could go to college without too great expense. The family income has dwindled to $3000, contributed by four members, of which the largest share is earned by the mother. The house they live in is rented and is not nearly so nice as their old one. In place of two expensive cars the family now has one second-hand Ford.

Mr. Burton is not the same happy, energetic

man that he was. The strain has made him very
nervous. "His attitude toward life has changed
from one of 'get the very most you can out of it' to
one of looking on life as a drudgery. Before he
moved he dropped out of his active participation
in the Knights Templar, the Y.M.C.A. and the
church; he did not feel he had the money to do the
things he was in the habit of doing for these
institutions. A few of his best friends stuck by
him, but all they did was offer him sympathy and
kind words. This hurt him, because, when prosperous, he was very generous; but when he lost his
money, no one helped him. He did not read as
much as before and he could no longer take a
whole-hearted interest in dancing or cards. His
friends therefore started to drop away. He still
however remains very kind and thoughtful toward
members of the family. It hurts him not to be able
to provide for his children, and especially, Elizabeth, in the way that he did before."

The mother has proven herself the family hero-
ine. She remains healthy, ambitious, vivacious,
while doing all the housework for her own family
and looking after the rooms for eight students, as
well as doing their washing and ironing. The
roomers are very fond of her and she does little
things for them such as making them midnight
lunches which they appreciate. She has given up
all her former social activities. She finds her life
completely within the home. Sometimes she gets

tired out and is a little cross with the family, but her children understand the load under which she is laboring and do not resent it.

Now and then she wishes for her old life but is on the whole contented. "She finds extreme pleasure in the little gifts such as flowers or candy which the boys in the house always give her on her birthday or before they go away on a vacation. Now and then one of the fellows will take her to a show, and she seems amply repaid for the little services she is always doing them. She sews a great deal for her own girls and she finds it extremely hard to refuse their requests. She has finally become reconciled to women smoking and has even gone the limit of saying that she would not care if her own daughters smoked as long as they told her."

The decrease has been easier for Lester to take than any of the rest. He never had spent much and so does not feel the change. Many of his home-town friends have come to the University and several of them live in the house. He is very much interested in a girl. His recreational center has shifted from the Y.M.C.A. to the university sports building. He is a junior and plans to enter the Law School. He works in a foundry in the summer and helps the family meet its budget. He is not so strict as he was and enjoys drinking beer very much. His parents do not like this, but he makes no secret of it. He is still quiet and unobtrusive, but his inferiority feelings are less marked. His antagonism toward his brother is largely gone, because he feels sorry for his brother's inability to make an adjustment. He is no more partial to his father now than to his mother and is more willing to enter into activities of the rest of the family.

Harry entered the Engineering School but did not do well and is staying out now, looking for work. He is still an easy-going, rather lazy young man, not too anxious to find a job. He does not read nor exercise, but the parents never say a harsh word to him. His former friends who are in the University have joined fraternities, and, since Harry cannot spend money as they do, they ignore him. He has not reconciled himself to the new situation and longs for the past. He is popular with the boys rooming in the house because of his pleasant personality.

Frances has been hit hard, and for much the same reason as Harry. It was difficult for her to give up her friendships and good times in Saginaw, but she has made a fairly successful adjustment. She is in high school and participates in club activities and enjoys dancing. She is attractive and has boys coming to take her out. She helps by working a few hours a week as a clerk in a store. She is sometimes stubborn and a little domineering at home, but she is likable nevertheless.

Elizabeth feels less badly about the decrease because she hardly realizes what she has missed. She is beginning to outgrow the results of early pampering. Her health is not good because of her inability to get enough sleep with noisy students about the house, and she is being kept out of school. She helps her mother considerably, especially with the washing and ironing. She has earned pin money looking after small children. She has many friends her own age and is very much interested in a sewing club that they have formed. She sometimes seems to delight in annoying her sister and she usually manages to get her mother's support in the little squabbles that occur.

The family feels that, despite the decline in their economic status, they are a more intellectual family than before, because the children, having no "society" ambitions now, are more concerned with school and college work. There is now no conflict within the family as to its cultural type, and this has removed the main source of friction. Lester's conception has won the day against that of Mrs. Burton, Harry, and Frances. The family is very isolated in Ann Arbor, having made almost no contacts with other residents.

The only cliques observable at all now are the two girls and the two boys in opposition to each other. Except for Frances, none of the children tries to dominate the family to the same degree as formerly, but they allow the natural leadership of the father and mother to assert itself. The children are doing much more around the house and doing it with a better spirit. Even Lester, who abhors such work, pitches in. Mrs. Burton is the principal leader, since she is both the chief earner and the chief buyer for the family. Mr. Burton's inferior position as an earner hurts him and he is ashamed that his wife has to work so hard, but he does not let this affect his attitude toward her.

The family members share their experiences and feelings more than before and are in general more sympathetic toward one another. They still adhere to birthday and holiday celebrations, and these are more anticipated and more spontaneously enjoyed. There is more thought of how each one's acts will affect the others and each no longer goes his separate way. The children feel more pride in their parents than formerly because they realize how steadfastly they have met the situation.

The Burton family was clearly only moderately integrated originally and the "society" ambitions of some of its members rendered it, seemingly, only moderately adaptable. That it did in fact prove quite remarkably flexible cannot influence our judgment regarding its original state, for we would then simply be deducing our facts from our theory.

The other two cases which are similar to No. 10 are No. 25 and No. 8. The former is a Jewish family living in New York in which there were six children, the oldest three of whom were earning and contributing to the family; the latter is a marine engineer's family from Erie in which the one child did not feel very close to his stepmother. In No. 25 the two principal breadwinners, the father and oldest son, found their family status somewhat altered when their incomes fell and those of other family members rose; in No. 8 the change of the father from a marine life to a job on shore modified the symbiotic positions of family members considerably, though the father remained the breadwinner. But this latter case will be discussed in more detail in Chapter XII. Case No. 25 shows in rather extreme form a very common result of such a decrease—loss of family pride and more unhappiness, in some members even bitterness, and at the same time more awareness of the necessity of helping each other and more willingness to do it. Case No. 8 also holds up well, so that all three show themselves readjustively invulnerable, though in No. 25 it is a close call.

Turning now to the effect of a changed-positions decrease on a Type V family, we will consider Case No. 2.

CASE NO. 2

The Wheeler family consisted of the father 57, mother 47, and three girls 24, 22, and 17. They lived in a 10-room house, which they had owned for 25 years, in one of the older residential areas of Indianapolis, an area upon which business was beginning to encroach. Mr. Wheeler was a factory foreman, having worked for the same company 30 years. His income was about $3000 before the decrease. The family owned two cars.

Mr. Wheeler's whole life revolved around his work and his family. His long employment amid the roar of machinery had rendered him a little deaf. He was ambitious for his family, but had himself fallen into a rut. He had always let his wife handle the family disbursements and he took no responsibility for managing the household. He was kindly, loyal and responsible both in his work and his family relations. "He was willing to work six months without pay to help the company through its most depressing time." He had a pleasant personality as a rule, but became very stubborn if nagged. He had set ideas about moral standards and was strict with the children.

He had had only 10 years of schooling but was competent with his hands and could fix anything, whether it required the skill of a carpenter, plumber, or mechanic. His chief enjoyments were his radio and fishing. He never cared much about visiting friends or driving about. He had always been a bit shy and timid. He did not spend much, but what he did spend was not budgeted and he sometimes left his wife with a problem on her hands to pay for his purchases. His few friends were men of his type and very loyal to him. Within his family he showed no favoritisms.

Mrs. Wheeler had lots of energy and ambition and the success of the children in getting an education was in large measure due to her. She had determined that all her daughters should have a college education and she was seeing to it that they got it. This responsibility had worn on her and she had become nervous as a result. For 3 years two girls had been in college together and the family's income had only been $250 a month. She had sacrificed everything for her children, always doing all her own work, wearing her clothes until threadbare. However, she was not unaware of the fact, and reminded the girls of it frequently. The latter resented this and considerable friction resulted. Her only activities outside the home were an occasional meeting of the Eastern Star and attendance at church. To her friends she had a very pleasant personality but at home she was likely to worry and become sulky and hard to live with. Her children felt sorry for her and yet sympathy on their part only encouraged her to emphasize her troubles the more. She was proud of the good records her girls had made in school, and perhaps inclined to favor the oldest a little, probably because she was more even-tempered than the others, and got along with her mother better.

Kathleen graduated from college 2 years before the decrease. She obtained a job teaching school

173

in Indianapolis and at this time was making $1400 a year, with bright prospects. She saved $1000 from her first 2 years' salary. Her particular concern was about her youngest sister's education and it was her hope to be able to help the latter develop her artistic talent. Kathleen was engaged to a young man not yet through his professional course in a university. She played bridge occasionally, but enjoyed more especially dancing and swimming. Her friends were mostly school teachers and college sorority sisters. Being very brilliant herself, she mingled with unusually intelligent people. Her greatest extravagances had been a fur coat and a trip to Florida during the summer vacation.

The second daughter, Sarah, was a tall, strong girl who also had made an enviable academic record. She entered college at 16 and specialized in art work. She had not intended to teach, but in the last year she had taken a few courses in the hope that she might be able to do so. However she did not have enough credits in education and was unable to secure a position. So she went back the following year and earned a life certificate. By then the depression had made positions scarce and the only one she could get was as a saleslady in a store.

She was rather unambitious, a little shy of trying conclusions with the world, and this brought much criticism on her head from her mother. She too was engaged, and she expected to get married shortly. Besides her art interests, she liked to swim and to attend plays, travel, dance, and otherwise enjoy lighter forms of amusement. She was thrifty, however, and made many of her own clothes. She had many college friends of rather an intellectual type, but had only a few close friends in Indianapolis. Sarah was not at all jealous of her more successful older sister, but was sometimes jealous of her younger one, who, she felt, was pampered by the rest.

Violet had been more or less sickly through her youth and did not have the energy of her older sisters. She was about to graduate from high school with high honors. She was a cheerful girl, alternately docile and fiery. Her main interest was also in art and she was accomplished for her age. She was looking forward with anticipation to college. She was not as economical as Kathleen and Sarah, but all during the time her sisters were in college she had had to wear old clothes made over for her, which may explain her desire to have nice things for herself. Her friends were of good families. She adored both of her sisters, but Sarah perhaps the more, because of their mutual art interests.

The family had worked out a pretty stable sort of organization and, with Mr. Wheeler's job apparently a life one, the future looked bright. There were three breadwinners—the father, Kathleen, and Sarah (although the latter's job was temporary), and they were saving. There were family functions occasionally, sometimes with relatives, and there was a strong consciousness of the family group. Joys and sorrows were shared to some extent, but the discipline of the parents was not always sympathetic.

The blow came when Mr. Wheeler was let out of his job without any warning. Within a week Sarah lost her sales position, so that the only income the family had was Kathleen's $1400 a year. Mr. Wheeler looked for other work but it soon became obvious that a man of his age could get nothing. The positions of the members have become radically changed. Mr. Wheeler is now around the house and is trying to assume the role of leadership there, probably as a compensation for his lost job. Since Mrs. Wheeler heretofore has had complete charge of the household and its finances, this is very upsetting.

Mr. Wheeler is not as good-tempered as he was, and he and his wife get into frequent quarrels over household matters. He tries to tell her how she should do things differently and this naturally produces resentment on her part. The relations in the home are very strained. He tries to keep busy by helping with the work at home, fixing screens, cleaning the cellar, even laying hardwood floors upstairs. But he thinks he knows better than his wife how these things should be done.

His friends have been kind to him but they

cannot find work for him. He finds almost no recreation now, even his radio being in need of repairs. At first he read up on steam boilers preparatory to taking civil service examinations for an inspector but he failed to pass the examination. He has been shaken from his rut, but he has found no new stabilizing force. He is greatly worried about his wife's and his own future and about their inability to send the youngest girl to the college of her choice.

Mrs. Wheeler is more worried and therefore more irritable than before. She nags her husband about his failure to hold or get a job. "Her mental attitude toward life has affected all her children to such a degree that at times it makes the entire tenor of life almost impossible to stand, and has been most depressing at all times. She never forgets what she has done for the family and it hurts her pride now when she realizes that, although she helped by saving, she wasn't the one who brought in the salary every month." She constantly states what she would have done if she had been her husband and says that they would not have let her out without her knowing the reason why. Her friends are sorry for her, but their sympathy only makes her feel her woes the more. She takes offense when any one suggests that she should not be so depressed. She seems not to appreciate the efforts the rest of the family make to ease her burdens. She never praises either her husband or her children and they resent this. She thinks they have never appreciated her.

Kathleen is holding her job and is unhappy because she feels she must support the family and cannot get married. She has had to give up a trip abroad which she had planned as a help to her teaching. She is very conscientious and realizes how much the family sacrificed for her education and she will not let them down. She is very economical now but manages to remain cheerful in spite of everything.

Sarah feels badly about her inability to keep a job and help the family out. She hopes to get married soon, as she is only an expense to the family. The loss of her job broke her morale, and now she has less ambition. She has been helping her mother at home and is really happier here than she was as a store clerk. "There is so much uncertainty in her life that she is in a constant turmoil and is gloomy a great share of the time. This changes when she leaves her jangling family and visits her fiancé." She still wants a nice wedding and is rather selfish in this respect.

The saddest tragedy of all revolves around Violet. She is just graduating from high school where she has won special mention for her art work. She is thought to have talent worth developing, but she has had to give up her idea of a university career. She is sweet and brave about it, but it hurts. All through high school she sacrificed things so that her sisters might have their college education. "Poor Violet was always the one who didn't have pretty clothes and the other sisters would say that she would have lots more than they when she went to college because she would be the only one in school. They built all sorts of air castles, and then when she couldn't go, and those air castles tumbled, there was sadness in all three sisters' eyes because they knew it wasn't fair." Violet, despite the fact that she has sacrificed the most, is the most cheerful of the family. She is going to a local college whose art department is inferior.

The relations between Mr. and Mrs. Wheeler are the center of all the family difficulties. If he could stop criticizing her ways of doing things and thus abate her bitter resentment toward his unemployment, the family could no doubt re-integrate itself satisfactorily. Every member is really sincerely concerned about the family situation, but this point of friction keeps the household upset. The children are trying to keep up the morale, but with only mediocre success. Even the work around the house does not elicit full co-operation because of sulkiness and bitterness on the part of the mother. Sarah is the only one to show selfishness, but even the others do not integrate their activities very well.

————

It hardly seems necessary to explain why the

original family situation was regarded as exemplifying Type V. The undercurrent of friction between mother and daughters justifies the "moderate integration" characterization, while the father's "being in a rut" indicates less than high adaptability. The lessening of integration after the decrease is paralleled very closely in the other Type V case meeting the changed-positions situation, case No. 36. This is the family used in Chapter III as the exemplar of this sort of decrease impact. There we found Mrs. York going to earn the family living as a bridge teacher when Mr. York's business failed. The father becomes a disturbing factor at home in both instances.

The fact seems to be that a family only moderately integrated and moderately adaptable cannot stand the complete loss of employment by the father, especially if he tries to make it up by assuming a different role in the home. The changed positions give rise to no satisfactory scheme of new family roles, and so the families prove vulnerable.

As was suggested at the beginning of this chapter there appears to be great similarity between Type V and Type II. The slightly less integration of the former seems to mean little as far as vulnerability is concerned. Indeed it will be recalled that one Type II family proved vulnerable to a modified-positions decrease. However, this was regarded as anomalous and it is now more apparent why, since all three type V families in a parallel situation emerged intact. One is forced to the general conclusion that even a moderate degree of adaptability will pull families with any integration at all through all but the worst crises.

CHAPTER IX

MODERATELY INTEGRATED, UN-ADAPTABLE FAMILIES

WITH this, our sixth type, we are again faced with incomplete evidence. Though we have five families in our series which seem to be properly classified here, four of them suffered a decrease with similar positions, while none of them represent the changed-positions situation.

Case No. 45 will be used to illustrate the impingement of a simple decrease on a moderately integrated, but unadaptable family.

CASE NO. 45

When the decrease came to the Watsons, the father was 54, the mother 56, Maud 22, Frank 21, Laura* 20, and Ernestine 14. They lived in a remodelled farmhouse on the edge of one of the fashionable suburbs of Chicago. Both Mr. and Mrs. Watson had come from wealthy families but had lost much of their money during their early married life and had come to Chicago to get a fresh start. Their neighbors were of the "four hundred" and, although they had nicer houses and much larger incomes (the Watsons' amounted to only $5200) they did not snub the latter. There were three cars in the family, two of them inexpensive second-hand ones used by the children. The mother and father were proud of rather aristocratic lineage and stressed the fact that the family members should remember that they were ladies and gentlemen.

At the time of the decrease Mr. Watson was the owner and manager of a machine shop which he had started a short time before. It had done very well and he expected soon to be "on easy street." He worked very hard and earned about $4000 a year. Though a college man, he felt a self-made man was more to be admired and rather doubted the value of his college training. He had few outside interests and was not religious. He was very strict with the children and insisted that they take his word as law. He gave them directions each night as to what he expected them to do the following day in the way of chores around the house and yard. He would not let the children play the phonograph while he was at home and refused to let them have a radio because it might interfere with the preparation of their lessons. He had no close friends and never went out evenings, even with Mrs. Watson. He belonged to no club or other organization.

Mrs. Watson was a quiet, thoughtful woman

who hardly dared to speak her own mind. Her main interest was her home and children and she did all she could to make life pleasant for them and to train them well. She was the mediator between her husband and the children and often smoothed the troubled waters. She had many friends and was very well liked. She missed the companionship which she did not receive from her husband but she did not talk about it. She seemed to fear her husband but she did not wish the children to realize that fear. She was a "thorough-bred with a broken spirit."

Maud was nervous, high strung, inclined to fits of depression and hard to live with. She had just recovered from a thyroid operation. In high school she had been an all-A student and was an honor student in college. "She seemed to lack interest in any kind of career and her leisure time was spent in sewing and reading. She was a member of the local church and participated in several religious organizations. Due to her physical condition she was unable to do any type of work and spent most of her time reading or closed in her own room, not desiring any other member of the family to accompany her. She had forgotten most of her high-school acquaintances and cared little about friendships during college. She seemed to possess a family spirit in that she always desired friendship with the other members, but was never able to enjoy their hobbies or interests and was extremely jealous of their good times and friendships with other companions." She was fussy and impatient of others' shortcomings.

Frank, 1 year younger than Maud, had just been dropped from college after 2 years of mechanical engineering. He was very skillful with his hands and had a mechanical bent which amounted almost to genius in fixing engines and the like, but was not bright academically and was a trifle lazy to boot. He was an easy-going sort who could be induced to work if praised. After leaving college he obtained a job in his father's shop where he had worked summers before. He got along well except for an occasional argument with his father. His chief interest was boats, especially sailboats. He would have left home any time for a job on a boat, and had, as a matter of fact, worked on a yacht as an oiler. He spent Saturday afternoons and Sundays sailing on Lake Michigan and he was much sought as a member of the crew by friendly yachtsmen. He had never managed to save his earnings and was extravagant in his gifts to girls. "His friends seemed to be selected from quiet, mouse-like people" mostly members of wealthy families in the neighborhood. He was always fixing things for them. He was closest to Laura and frequently sided with her against Maud.

Laura was large for her age, healthy and lively. She desired to be a teacher. She had been a leader in all high-school activities and graduated with honor. After working 2 years as a church secretary earning $1000 a year, she entered a local college on the money saved. She was especially interested in all outdoor activities. Her friends were mainly those made during high school, though she had many acquaintances in college. She had never been close to either of her sisters. She felt that Maud pried too much into her affairs, exaggerated her actions in reporting them to their mother, and was jealous of her friendship with other girls. Laura liked to dance but Maud disliked her going out. She moved in the same circle as Frank and they were much together. Ernestine was too young to have much in common with her.

Ernestine was finishing junior high school at this time. She was pretty, had a very pleasant personality, and was interested in swimming, skating and other sports. She was only a mediocre student. She was not interested in boys but had many girl friends. The family had spoiled her somewhat. She showed no jealousy of the others, however.

The father and mother had a strong sense of social status and forbade the children to play with those beneath them socially. Frank and Laura were reprimanded frequently for their interest in peddlers and other unconventional people. The neighbors thought the family quite ideal, but they did not realize the lack of true companionship within the family circle.

Mr. Watson, as has been indicated, believed in a patriarchal family organization. He told each of the others what to do, where to go, how to spend the money he doled out, and even insisted that the children turn in their earnings to him. Maud accepted the situation and enjoyed her father's confidence, but Frank and Laura frequently rebelled. Mrs. Watson was the influence that kept these two from kicking over the traces entirely. The only common activities were swimming, which all the members enjoyed, and events like the father-and-son banquet, at which the mother and girls waited on table, and the mother-and-daughter banquet at which the father and son did likewise. All but the father went to Sunday School or church. The family never went riding in the automobile as a group. Annually the members would, however, get together in redecorating the house before the visit of relatives. When the three older children were all going to college there was considerable co-operation among them, but Laura and Maud could not get along at home when they tried to co-operate on a dress for Ernestine.

Mr. Watson was cruel in his discipline, resorting to whipping on occasion. The children, however, felt Mrs. Watson's reprimands more keenly because they realized it hurt her to have to scold them. She was sympathetic and tried to keep them from incurring her husband's wrath.

It was Mr. Watson's idea that all the children

should ultimately come into the shop—the girls to be stenographers and Frank to succeed to the managership. He had, however, relented sufficiently to allow Maud and Laura to go to college. Mrs. Watson secretly encouraged all of them to develop their own bents and as a result Maud had considerable aptitude in designing clothes, Laura wanted to teach, and Ernestine to become a swimming instructor.

The decrease in this family came very sharply. The business of the shop fell off rapidly and the father's income was practically wiped out. Frank had been forced to leave college just before and now Maud and Laura were withdrawn from college too. The former took the place of Mr. Watson's office girl soon after. The family moved to a small six-room house and sold two of the cars. The yard is no longer well kept up.

Mr. Watson had one fixed idea—to save the shop. He "clings to the belief that some wealthy person will become interested and invest enough money to put it on its feet. Unless conditions change rapidly he cannot hold on more than another 6 months, but refuses to believe that it cannot be saved. He has devoted 6 years to the shop and has built dreams and hopes for his reward in old age. He wants the family circle complete and thinks that all owe it to him to remain single and devote their energies to the fast sinking ship." He is not insured, has sugar diabetes and must frequently contemplate suicide. He is more strict than ever with the children. He now listens a great deal to the radio, insists on choosing the programs and drives the rest of the family nearly frantic with his choices. He objects to company and never calls on any one. He has become intensely interested in the NRA, attends every local meeting, and hopes that it will prove the salvation of his business.

Mrs. Watson is a changed person. She is "irritable, nagging, constantly 'singing the blues.'" She goes out more than formerly, is now active in the Ladies Aid and seems to desire to be away from the family difficulties. At home she is very quiet and often she and her husband do not exchange more than a sentence or two in an evening. "She is discouraged and unhappy. Money is scarce and pleasant words scarcer. She seems to be undecided as to just what is best for the children or herself."

Maud, since she went to work as her father's office girl, has definitely aligned herself with her father. She has also adopted his contempt for college education. Once an all-A student herself, she now thinks professors are prolonging the depression and that college life is the root of all evil.

Her physical health has improved, but she is not easier to get along with. She is more set in her ways and even less tactful than formerly.

She shows no interest in any recreations, rarely reading and never going out. She has given up any notion of a separate career and seems to be perfectly content with her job.

Frank has changed very little. He would like to leave the shop and seek employment elsewhere, but he does not for two reasons: He could probably not get employment now and, even if he could, he dreads the family row that would ensue if he left. His check each month is divided, most of it going to his mother for family expenses and the remainder being given to him. He accepts his lot without rebellion and, as long as he can sail in the summer, he is quite contented. He still plays around with successive "girls."

Laura has broken openly with the family. She had a summer job as playground director in 1931 and was determined to go on with her college career on part of the proceeds. Her father demanded that she turn it all in for family expenses. She refused, and left for the University of Michigan where she obtained a board and room job doing housework. This enraged her parents who felt that she was smudging the family escutcheon by "demeaning herself" to do housework for some one else. Since then she has been completely self-supporting and has not returned home. She never hears from her father, only occasionally from her mother. Maud has kept up a correspondence with her, however. Laura is much happier than she has ever been and finds her new-found freedom wonderful. She has just married a college man.

Ernestine is graduating from high school but her grades are not good enough for her to be recommended for college. She, like Laura, hates the shop and will not go near it. She has a summer teaching job in a local Bible School at $5 a week and in the afternoon runs a nursery for nearby children. She goes out with boys but does not confide in any member of the family concerning her affairs. This worries Maud, but Ernestine is the apple of her father's eye and he does not mind her reaction against the shop nor her desire to go out. She is the only one of the children who has been given any freedom at home.

The clique between Maud and her father is very marked. Mrs. Watson used to say "we think" but now it is "they think." They dominate the household. The pride in ancestry is not so much spoken of now. The members confide in each other even less than before. Maud and Ernestine especially fail to understand each other, although they share the same bedroom. Mr. Watson and Frank have frequent spats over the hour of his return at night. The members remaining at home are united in one way, however—they all regard Laura as a black sheep because of her housework job and because she has married the son of a factory employee. The old "we" feeling has almost disappeared. The children think of themselves rather than of each other.

———

The propriety of classifying the Watson family originally as moderately integrated and unadaptable can be defended by emphasizing their internal dissensions despite a good deal of family pride on the one hand, and the dogged and uncompromising dominance of the father on the other. A family ruled by an autocrat with a fixed idea is the very acme of rigidity. After the decrease in income the situation became intolerable and the family solidarity plainly weakened.

The three remaining families of this group were judged unadaptable because of the combination of materialistic outlook and a high standard of living. The results in all three are highly interesting, and two of the cases, No. 5 and No. 26, are treated in detail among the special cases in Chapter XII. In Case No. 5, which was used in Chapter III to illustrate Type VI, things remained about the same. The mother and grandmother began doing the housework, but affection and community of interests fell off, if anything. A similar indeterminate result characterizes Case No. 26. Case No. 27 shows us a large family of six children in a small town, the father of proud English lineage, the wife a capable, reckless woman who was at one time a railway telegrapher. There was a loose family organization before the decrease and the members had no thought but to spend money irresponsibly on pleasure. The impact of the decrease did not lessen the family's solidarity, but neither did it bring to the fore any unsuspected sources of cohesion. Thus we are led to conclude that the critical point for Type VI families lies somewhere in the middle of the similar-positions range, for one of the families proved firmly invulnerable to this type of pressure, one proved vulnerable, and in two cases it is an open question whether the family can be said to have broken under the strain.

Let us turn now to our single instance of a decrease with modified positions among the Type VI cases—No. 44.

CASE NO. 44

The Lacroix family are French-Canadian in ancestry, though the parents have lived in this country since their marriage. Just prior to the decrease the ages of those at home were as follows: Mr. Lacroix 70, Mrs. Lacroix 67, Pierre 29, Helene* 25, and Rose 22. They had been living in Detroit for eleven years. Previously they had lived in the "copper country of Northern Michigan." At this time they occupied a large six-room apartment equipped with all modern conveniences, renting for $100 a month. The neighborhood contained many apartment buildings of about the same class. In the home were a piano and a combination radio and phonograph, and the family owned a car. The apartment was tastefully but not expensively decorated. Just before the decrease, with four members working, the income was approximately $7000.

Mr. Lacroix worked intermittently as a construction foreman, receiving about $1800. He had at one time drawn a good salary which had made possible some saving, but he had not worried much about a rainy day, believing that his children should support his wife and himself in their old age. At this time he regarded his work as temporary and felt little obligation to continue. He felt he was doing the rest a favor to work at all. His chief interests were "politics, his pipe and the radio." He spent very little, but it was from lack of desire rather than motives of economy. Whenever he really wanted anything he got it. He had very few friends and saw little of those few. He enjoyed talking to other members of the family. Political issues were his favorite topics of discussion, though he also liked to talk about odd items of all sorts which he read in the papers. His knowledge was extensive considering the little formal education he had had. He showed no affection toward his wife, nor did she toward him. The children gave him a rather grudging affection which he returned in an undemonstrative way.

Mrs. Lacroix was suffering from a goitre but was mentally happy, resting in the assurance of a steady income and feeling that her children were established after a long, hard struggle on her part. The last few years had been the only period of her life in which she could relax and enjoy life a little. "Her one ambition had been to have her youngest daughter, who suffered curvature of the spine, independent. This was realized. She relapsed sometimes into a youthfulness to which the members of the family were unaccustomed and which was pleasantly surprising to them. She had visions of expanding a bit and doing kind things for others less fortunate. Her philosophy was that of the hard-working, courageous individual who is at last reaping the rewards of honesty, frugality, rigid morality, and kindliness. Also she rested happy in the love and loyalty of her children."

Pierre, at this time 29, was not strong physically and was a trifle dull mentally. He had been socially rather inadequate all through his youth and perhaps had over-compensated somewhat. More than anything else he enjoyed mechanical work. He had left school promptly on his sixteenth birthday against the wishes of the family, had obtained a job, and become financially independent—even a contributor to the support of the family. This was tonic to him—it bolstered his self-respect, gave him a source of satisfaction, made his life purposeful. He was left to take care of his mother and younger sisters." (None of the family leaned on the father, who worked sporadically.) Pierre developed a sense of self-sufficiency and pride he had never had before. "He even spoke of everything as 'his.' It was 'his' house, 'his' radio, 'his' car." This was a bit annoying at times, but seemed to be clearly understood by the others for what it was worth. He made about $2000 a year during the boom period, more than his father or his married brothers. "He was on a par with them at last. His work meant everything to him. It was his forte. He made very few friends—in fact he did not even make friends within the family. His object in life was to care for his mother." His recreations were attendance at theatres, baseball games, circuses, state fairs, and other similar events. "He could afford to go where he pleased and managed to see a great deal. He dressed well, bought a car, joined a lodge, banked money and bought a lot. He was thinking that some day he would travel." All this had given him a self-sufficiency and integration which made him a little cocksure and overbearing at times. He wished to dominate the rest and usually opposed suggestions made by other family members. By this stubborn, unintelligent resistance he compensated for his real inadequacy. In the early days he had pooled his wages with the family's but in the last few years had merely paid for room and board.

Helene had not enjoyed good health for some time before the decrease. During adolescence she had been under-weight to the point of emaciation and just prior to the depression had been operated on for hyper-thyroidism. She had always been extremely nervous and quick-tempered. She was constantly consciously controlling nervous reactions. Her outlook was not healthy either, for she felt life futile. She was sincere, active, studious and had many friends, but she was unhappy and dissatisfied because she felt they were on a lower plane than she, a plane to which she descended in associating with them. She was therefore retiring more and more into herself.

Her high-school studies had been a source of great pleasure to her. She had projected herself into college and imagined herself ultimately an author, travelling to the ends of the earth. The family did not share these aspirations. She was to be a business woman. To her this "was the closing of the door." She went into business as a stenographer, prejudiced against it in advance. Although she was efficient and got along well, she hated it and despised the lack of idealism and superficial interests of those with whom she came in contact. She changed jobs to try to find a more congenial atmosphere, but in vain. She felt responsibility for her frailer younger sister who would have to be seen through college, and therefore she dared not quit her job. In order to attain some sort of adjustment, she went to dances, bought a fur coat and otherwise let herself be carried with the crowd. But she rather despised it all and wished she were in college. She was becoming neurotic when her employer insisted on medical care, and the operation ensued. She resumed her job, her health much improved, at $1800 a year, but still she was dissatisfied with her lot.

Rose, the youngest, had suffered keen mental torture from her physical handicap of spinal curvature incurred at 14. Helene was her only confidante and she withdrew completely from her high-school classmates. College found her much happier, with friends both male and female. She found subjects she enjoyed and she received appreciation, but she always remained more or less dependent upon Helene. They became very close and she understood Helene's desire to get away from her business life. When she graduated from college she found a fine library position suitable to her temperament and became happy in it. Her income was $1500 a year. She made a few friends of her own, but she depended mostly on Helene's friends for companionship. The two sisters went to theatres together, read together, played the piano and sang together. They shared everything, even their incomes. Rose remained, however, shy, timid, and wistful.

The father and mother had not become assimilated to American life and their friends were almost exclusively French-Canadians like themselves. They also had rather materialistic ambitions. Their older children (those married and Pierre) shared this point of view, with the result that the two younger girls found their ideals in sharp conflict with those of the rest of the family. The children understood the parents, but the parents did not understand the two younger girls.

The mother dominated the family group more than any other member. The children felt a strong sense of loyalty toward her, but not much toward the father, whose irresponsibility was resented. The children felt that all they had received was due to their mother. She was regarded as a martyr. Being of a melancholy type, she dominated through the sympathy which she aroused in her children. There was a good deal of family feeling but the family was never really happy. This was probably due to the lack of affection between the father and mother. "The mother clung to her children—wanted to order their lives in the minutest detail. However, she felt secure in her little circle. She had succeeded in stopping any further 'leaves' or breaks through marriage and felt that nothing could break it. There was financial security and no one was engaged. What more could she ask?"

The two girls felt their unity as incompatible with that of the family. They dreamed of having an apartment together "and of course bringing

199

mother along." But the father and the brother were felt to be in a hostile camp.

Despite all this the family had considerable solidarity based on custom and tradition. Though the children might feel bound, still they felt the family ties. There were family occasions such as picnics and long Sunday afternoon drives, and holiday celebrations. The mother opposed separate activities. But there was no general sharing of hopes, joys, sorrows. The mother had no insight into the inner lives of her children and felt that if they had material comforts they should be satisfied.

The family members did not appropriate opportunities selfishly, but there was no general family desire for all to have the best opportunities possible for development. The father and mother particularly saw no use in higher education.

The depression soon found three of the four wage earners out of work completely—the father, Pierre, and Helene. Rose was the only one to hold her job. The father was expected to stop work in a few years anyway, so that this was not so upsetting. But Pierre and Helene had been counted on as the very pillars of the family's existence.

Mr. Lacroix is almost unaffected. Loss of income means nothing to him. He was glad to give up the responsibility of work. He has no conception of the problems of the rest. He sleeps, smokes his pipe and listens to the radio and is interested in the present economic situation as an academic matter only.

Mrs. Lacroix is "infinitely older, frailer, worried, harassed, heart broken—a bit hardened, but indomitable. She had met much adversity which had given her quite a tendency to look on the dark side—now this comes to the fore. But there is a new spirit shining out—it is the feeling that she doesn't care. She is old, there is no use in fighting. She has given everything. She has nothing more to give. She is just anxious for the end. Her new worry is about her son. He is rather frail—has no mental or physical resources to fall back upon in the face of adversity. She has also lost faith in the loyalty of some of her children who, in the face of their own prosperity, can allow her to bear this burden of worry." (These are married children.) "She lives from day to day, working out her frugal budget joylessly, uninterestedly, when she really should be receiving the care of a trained nurse. The toll in the health, happiness and peace of mind of this member of the family has been great."

Pierre's "front" has been washed away by the depression. "He is physically much frailer. He has aged considerably. He has completely lost his *role*. He is unable to face what he considers an exposure. He considers himself a failure. His inadequacy stands revealed to himself. He has previously sensed it, but never actually experienced it. Without his shield of a good job he cannot face the rest of the world. Occasionally he "talks big" but has lost all his braggadocio. Very often he talks deprecatingly of himself. Sometimes he will sit for hours and do nothing but stare. He lacks initiative of any sort. He hates activity of any kind, hates to look for work.

"Sometimes he will tirade against every one—the government, church, home, friends. One feels a tension, a conflict, a strain when he is about. Sometimes when this strain is too great he 'goes to pieces' in a most pitiable, horrible way. All his inhibitions, his restraints, are lifted and he reveals all his hurts, his disappointments, frustrations—till it is more than others can bear. He once became involved in such a scene in the presence of several young nieces. All the children were weeping and utterly torn with sympathy. He is now incapable of making the least decision for himself—for instance, to wear or not to wear a coat is a source of conflict.

"He has, however, made a few friends. They come over and play bridge or talk depression (mildly)." He has acquired somewhat of an interest in books and likes to listen to political and economic discussions on the radio. This is a side of him which school never succeeded in stimulating.

Pierre does much of the housework, though he detests it. He is easier to live with in one sense—he is more considerate and sociable.

Helene was hurt by the loss of her good position. It was her first experience with failure. The shock was cruel because she instantly felt that the depression was not temporary, but a real, lasting thing. "Whoever was out of a job now would continue to *be* without one. Her mind grasped instantly for college."

It took her about four months to decide on this step, however, since she was much more deliberate than formerly (due to the slowing down of all her reactions from the operation). "The readjustments [at college]—in working habits, in social habits, in living habits—were rather tremendous, but she was doing what she wanted to do. She has acquired a decisiveness, a power, a certainty of manner and speech which she never had. Life is no longer futile. Life is interesting—an absorbing experience. She hopes to write, but is training to teach. She has a new hope for the future—nothing seems impossible. She has an optimism and faith which are surprising to her. She is on her way!

"She spends very little money—only for essentials—seldom for amusements. She has a slight income of $5 a week when in school. She had a mere $500 and an insurance policy when she faced college life. She has maintained a *B* average and been highly encouraged by several of her professors to go on."

Rose "is bearing the financial brunt of the depression. She has become the encourager and mainstay of all. Also she has developed independence—emotional and social. She has, however, become *tired*. She is nervous, quick-tempered (where she had no temper before). She is no longer dependent upon her older sister—she has made a great number of friends. She spends her money more prodigally than before—since the bank holiday she has a feeling of 'What's the use of saving? some one else will get your money in the end.' She is still quite generally loved and prized by the immediate family and her friends. She is quite anxious to see that her sister gets the thing she wants. She has a faith in her which is most stimulating to the other."

The family has maintained its social status during the depression—in fact it is now considered of a little more intellectual type than before because of the second daughter's going to college. The morale of the family is pretty low but appearances are kept up and the family is better off than many of its neighbors. "The family circle is not what it was." Helene does not think of the others as much as formerly, but looks out for her own future. She is not so close to Rose who has become the superior one of the pair where she was formerly the inferior. This translation of roles was not achieved without some friction and bitterness.

The father is regarded by the rest as a failure and is silently blamed for their misfortunes. Occasionally he flinches a bit under the implied criticism in their attitude. He now feigns illness as a defense. Pierre has a depressing effect on the family. He is pitied but this does not prevent his creating a strained air in the home.

There are still common activities and there is perhaps a greater willingness to take others into one's confidence and probably more sympathy for each other's plight.

———

It hardly seems necessary to defend the placement of this family as it originally was in Type VI. Integration was moderate to say the least, and the irresponsible attitude of the father and the somewhat unsound adjustment of the son rendered its adaptability very meager. When the decrease came there was intelligent readjustment of their lives by some of the family members, but it would seem that the family is not meeting the problem adequately as a family, and that the structure has proven itself definitely vulnerable to the impact. This family would probably have fared even worse if the father had been the chief breadwinner or the dominant family figure in the first place. Indeed if he had been, we would have been forced to regard the situation as one of changed rather than modified positions. Since he was not, he has not felt the modification of positions much—and one may interpret the results here as showing shifts of positions, without corresponding and adequate shifts of role. The family members are performing different functions but they do not make even as much of a whole as they did originally.

Type VI families are weak in just the same way that Type III ones were. Lack of adaptability certainly spells defeat in a contest with a severe pressure, and even a simple decrease is too much for some of the families of this type. It is worth noting, however, that the lower degree of integration, as compared with Type III, makes these families, apparently, no more poorly prepared than highly integrated, unadaptable ones to meet a decrease.

CHAPTER X

UNINTEGRATED, MODERATELY ADAP-
TABLE FAMILIES

IT will be recalled that our series showed no
families that were unintegrated and yet highly
adaptable. If our scheme were perfectly sym-
metrical and logically complete it would contain
such a type. Our approach however has been inductive throughout and we therefore ignore the
possibility that further research might reveal such
families, and denote as Type VII the unintegrated,
moderately adaptable families. It may be worth
noting in passing that we would expect unintegrated, highly adaptable families to be very rare
in any event, since the two conditions come close
to being contradictory. Families which are very
loosely organized are almost inevitably families in
which there is irresponsibility with respect to
group obligations and this would interfere with
adaptability; while highly adaptable families could
hardly have achieved these qualities without a
moderate measure of integration.

In Type VII we have three cases only—No. 31,
No. 46, and No. 17. The first experienced a similar-positions decrease and the last two a changed-

positions one. It should be recalled at this point that study of these Type VII cases and the single Type VIII case led us to the conclusion that the concept of vulnerability was not applicable to unintegrated families because they had not sufficient structure to buttress their external shell. In the scale of pressures there does not seem to be a critical point at which a cracking takes place. The families are too amorphous to begin with. Hence we cannot deal with these cases in as precise a way as those falling in the previous types. We can merely describe and comment upon the manner in which the different pressures have reacted upon these formless entities. Case No. 31 gives us the picture for the slight pressure of a simple decrease.

CASE NO. 31

The McMillan family is highly religious, and of Scotch-Irish heritage. It is composed of five members, who at the time of the decrease were of the following ages: father 43, mother 42, John* 19, Estelle 16, and Hilton 11. They lived in a middle-class district of Detroit. Their house was a moderate-sized wooden one and the family had a medium-priced car and a radio. Mr. McMillan owned and ran a trucking business and his income was about $4500 a year. He was generally cheerful and optimistic but likely to fly off the handle when irrritated. He had been slightly deaf for many years but this affliction was gradually getting worse, so that he was becoming very sensitive about it. He was energetic and always honest and sincere in his dealings. The more sociable forms of recreation were not attractive to him and he liked best to fish and hunt. He was also interested in archery. His friends were few but intimate. He was frugal in his expenditures and did not encourage the children to spend more than was absolutely necessary. In matters of conduct too he was strict with them, though he inclined to favor the daughter a little. He was hard for the children to know, for he kept them somewhat at a distance.

Mrs. McMillan had not been in good health since the birth of the youngest child, for she suffered from a bad heart and asthma. She was therefore unable to do very much in addition to her housework. Always kindly, perhaps even indulgent towards the children, she favored John a little. Outside of her home the church was her chief interest and it was there that she made many of her friends. Others were wives of Mr. McMillan's business associates and girlhood chums. She tried to bring up the children to be good Christians.

John was perhaps inclined to be a little selfish and found it hard to get along with his brother and sister. He was then in a local college, only a mediocre student, and inclined to "get by" on as little work as possible. He was particularly interested in girls, and "dates" were his chief form of recreation. He also liked sports and camping. In high school he had played a violin in the orchestra. He was frugal in connection with expenditures for lunches, but extravagant on "dates." His "best girl" was a daughter of a minister and perhaps that was the reason for his ambition to enter a medical school and become a medical missionary. He had also participated much in the young people's work at church. His chores around the house consisted in keeping the basement clean, emptying the ashes and filling the ice-box. He did these things regularly, not from any strong sense of duty but because he found this the easiest course.

Estelle "was a healthy girl. She was inclined to be dissatisfied with her clothing, chiefly because she associated with girls whose parents could provide them with better clothes. She was very conscious of the size of her feet. She was difficult to get along with. Her chief hobby was swimming. She did not belong to any particular group. Her friends were largely those with whom she came in contact at school, and one or two girls in the neighborhood." The fact that she never had any "dates," while her brother did, galled her, and she made it unpleasant at home on this account. She would sometimes go into temper tantrums. Her discontent was a constant source of unhappiness in the home. She compensated for her social maladjustment by making a striking academic record.

Hilton was quick-tempered and strong-willed and inclined to do as he liked except when he found himself in opposition to his father. He would side first with John and then with Estelle in the two latter's quarrels. He was often mean and his friends were not of a type to make him improve in this regard. He was easily led and had no particular hobby of his own. He had no regular duties to be performed at home.

There was much hypocrisy in the behavior of the children toward each other when there were guests. Then they were model children. But really there was deep antagonism and jealousy. Whenever one got new clothes, the others raised a fuss; they squabbled over washing the dishes, and in general showed no family spirit.

What organization there was in the family was due to the domination of the father. However, Mrs. McMillan did not always accept this domination without protest. The most obvious split in the family was between two cliques—father and daughter *vs.* mother and John. Hilton was a shifting factor. The only integrating forces were the church, which was attended by all, and the family holiday celebrations. Christmas was celebrated with other relatives as a clan affair. There was, however, almost no sharing of problems. The parents wanted their children to have opportunities, but they did not succeed in bringing about a home life which was very conducive to development.

The impingement of the decrease was in this case a simple, uncomplicated reduction to $1500 in the father's income, with no changes in position.

Mr. McMillan has become more kindly and sympathetic, both toward members of his family and others who are suffering more severely than he from the depression. The situation seems to have brought out a latent kindliness in him. He is at the same time more pessimistic about business and government. "There is less favoritism in his treatment of the children. He has tried to be cheerful at home even though business is bad. The fact that he owns his own business and consequently feels every loss very keenly has a depressing effect. He has learned the dangers of buying on credit and swears that if things ever get normal again he will pay cash for everything.

Mrs. McMillan has become kinder and more loving, though, since there was less room for improvement to begin with, this is not so noticeable as with the father. She has helped with the business by serving as bookkeeper and at the same time has continued to do most of her housework. "She has become more active socially both at church and outside of church life. Her health has not improved any. She has been a very important factor in maintaining the group morale."

John transferred from the local college to the

University of Michigan soon after the decrease and has worked his way since. He has found this experience very worth while. He is more self-reliant, helpful, cheerful and sincerely religious. He appreciates the other members of his family more than before and gets along better with his brother and sister. The number of his friends has grown and he is somewhat wiser in his expenditures. He has not been as active in organizations as before, but he has shown marked ability to adjust under conditions very different from those he was accustomed to. He has become rather critical of others who do not prove equally adaptable.

Estelle has become prettier and is more popular with boys. She is therefore not so jealous of her brother. However she still goes with a crowd the members of which have more money to spend than she, so that she is inclined to be extravagant in her expenditures. She makes up for this somewhat by being more helpful around the house. She has done much of the housework since her mother went to work in the office. She has been highly successful in school. The cost of her clothes is the chief bone of contention remaining between her and her brothers. Her social activities center around the church.

Hilton seems happier too since the decrease. He is in many activities in church and school and has begun a stamp collection in which he is much interested. He has been given the chores that John used to do when living at home, but he does not do them as regularly.

The family organization is closer than formerly. There is less domination and more real leadership. Mr. and Mrs. McMillan get along better with one another and the children have lost most of their mutual jealousies. "There is a much prouder sense of 'we.' "

———

The McMillans were originally classified as unintegrated because of the severe antagonisms and well-defined cliques which seemed to exist. When one sees the result one is led to wonder whether the student who described his family was not painting the picture a little too darkly.[1] There is another confusing factor here also. The decrease can hardly be blamed for all the change. The fact that Estelle became better looking, for instance, seems to have removed one cause of friction with her brother, since it meant that she went out more and was therefore less envious of his good times. In short, there are a number of considerations which make No. 31 an imperfect illustration of a "pure" Type VII case subjected to the pressure of a decrease with similar positions. However, it would appear a safe conclusion that moderate

[1] As a matter of fact when Mr. Fuller made an independent classification of these families he placed this one in Type V, thus showing that I was perhaps mistaken in my assignment. Its reactions are certainly very like those of Type V families.

adaptability can at least prevent an unintegrated family from becoming any worse under these circumstances.

Turning now to our two Type VII cases which experienced the severe pressure of changed positions, we take No. 17 as our example, since we have already used No. 46 to illustrate the meaning of our types in Chapter II.

CASE NO. 17

The Rileys have two children who were, at the time of the decrease, 24 and 17. Mr. Riley was 53 and his wife 45. Winifred was the older child and Michael the younger. They lived in a small Michigan town. Their house was a wooden one which they rented, and was located in the best residential district of the town. There was very little yard and no garden. Most of the furniture was worn and shabby, but there was a radio and piano. The family spent more money for books and magazines than for furnishings. The family had never owned their own home but had rented several houses, none of which had been well kept up or neatly cared for.

Mr. Riley was a tall, thin, nervous person, brilliant, but extremely self-centered, and was lazy. He neglected his law practice which would otherwise have been good, for he was recognized as a very clever man. He led a very irregular life, drinking as many as 20 cups of coffee a day and sleeping only four hours a night. Since he read constantly, he knew a little about almost everything. He was in debt thousands of dollars and still spent extravagantly. He was affable and generous with his money. Though his income was only $2800, he lived well, belonged to clubs, and did or purchased whatever he wanted. He was an enthusiastic golfer and nature lover. His friends ranged from high political figures to pool-room loafers. He had never taken much interest in his family, neglecting his wife shamefully and never helping to bring up the son. The daughter, who was an accomplished singer, received more attention from him, probably because she reflected some glory upon him.

Mrs. Riley was a calm, intelligent woman, attractive in appearance. She had a rather easygoing attitude toward life too, though not to the same degree that her husband had. She was very likable and entertaining to be with. Her principal interest was directing her daughter's voice training and musical career. She was her daughter's accompanist and went with her everywhere, sometimes being away from home three or four months at a time. Her income from accompanying other musicians was about $200 a year. She was more careful in her expenditures than her husband. Her friends were the wealthy, educated women of the community. She had centered her interest on the daughter with the result that the son had grown up without much attention. She and her husband were not close companions and she seemed to feel little obligation toward him or the home.

Winifred was a tall, attractive girl whose health was not very good but who had a great deal of energy and ambition. She was temperamental in the typical *artiste* manner. Though really selfish, she seemed charming and gracious to outsiders. Her vocal career shared her attention with numerous love affairs. She was well read and had travelled extensively both in the United States and Europe. She was bright but immature in many ways and depended almost wholly on her mother for guidance. "She had a rather detached attitude toward her father and brother." Her income at this time was only about $300 a year. She was very extravagant in her personal expenditures. She had numerous friends among the ranks of well-known musicians. She did not help at all with the housework when at home.

Michael was a tall, well-built boy with handsome features. His heart was none too strong and he was not particularly energetic. He was rather placid and carefree in temperament, well liked by both boys and girls. He was president of his high-school fraternity and the girls were eager for "dates" with him. His principal interest in high school was in the athletic teams, though he was bright enough when he wanted to work on his academic subjects. He was also editor of a high-school newspaper. His friends were sons and daughters of the wealthier people of the community. Considering his neglect at home, he was turning out remarkably well. He assumed a large share of the household duties and was careful in his own expenditures, though generous to a fault.

The family considered itself and was considered by the community to be an intellectual and artistic, if somewhat erratic, one. The members were received in the town's best social circles.

As has been implied, there was almost no family organization. The mother exerted more unifying influence than any one else, but that was little enough. There was not, however, any particular jealousy. Michael, who might well have been jealous of his sister, seemed to accept the greater attention lavished on her as natural. There were no common activities shared by all the members. Aside from the close mother-daughter relationship, there was very little intimacy among the family members. There was no discipline. And yet in spite of all this the family members were proud of their family and of the achievements of its members.

A position change accompanied the decrease in this case because, as the father's income went steadily down, that of his daughter went steadily up, so that she became the chief breadwinner. He neglected his practice more and more.

Mr. Riley has seemingly lost what little balance he had. "He spends his entire time in the town's worst pool room, playing cards with the lowest 'riff-raff' of the community. His income has dropped to about $900 a year. He is even more nervous than before and seems to be absolutely unmoved by the terrible condition of his finances. He spends as much as before or rather charges it. He is genial and amiable and reads a great deal, as before. He has retained his old friends, but they are worried about him, for it seems certain that he is headed toward financial disaster, and perhaps toward insanity. In his home he is much the same, except that he is more genial and seems more interested in his family, especially in the daughter.

Mrs. Riley has not quite the same influence over Winifred that she had before the latter became the chief breadwinner. She has, however, benefitted from Winifred's generosity, because the latter has purchased many little pleasures and luxuries for her. She "has entered somewhat into the social life of her friends and now attends many more parties and meetings of clubs than she did formerly, probably due to a need for new interests since her daughter's dependence is lessened. She seems to be little concerned by her husband's nervous condition and his financial difficulties. She seems absolutely independent of him and to expect her daughter to provide for her support if his is entirely withdrawn. Her son seems to have a growing interest for her, but it has not developed to any great extent. She and her husband seem to be widely separated. Her home is slightly more neat and clean than it was before, probably because of her daughter's wishes."

Winifred has become somewhat cynical about her family since they have not scrupled to live off her income. This income has increased to roughly a thousand dollars a year. Her health is no better but she is more mature and takes a more serious view of life. She is scornful of her father, more independent of her mother, and much more interested than formerly in her brother. She is now trying to do all she can to further his education and career.

Michael is the only one in the family who really worries about the family's situation. He is still in high school and doing well. He is the only one who has any sympathy for his father; he plays golf with him and is now closer to him than before. He hopes to take a medical course in college, which will be made possible by an uncle.

Winifred has become more of a family leader, while the leadership of the mother has been weakened, and whatever influence the father formerly had is now completely gone. Michael gets a little more consideration than before. In some ways stronger, in other ways weaker, the family must be regarded as having about the same degree of integration.

———

That this case was originally of the Type VII variety needs little proof. The lack of integration is all too obvious, while the moderate degree of adaptability is indicated by the queer combination of indifference and resourcefulness which characterizes the family. The decrease itself compels one to make a difficult decision between modified and changed positions, but the latter seems preferable because of the moral as well as pecuniary downfall of the father. The results illustrate in a clear way the contention that unintegrated families cannot be thought of as vulnerable or invulnerable. They are merely pushed this way or that by the forces that strike them, like a derelict. It is only seaworthy ships that can properly be regarded as possessing the quality of vulnerability or its opposite.

The other case which illustrates the same process, No. 46, shows a like inconclusive outcome. There we find a continued insistence on the part of the children that they live their own lives and an increased bitterness toward their father for not having helped with their education, but at the same time a growing sense of responsibility toward the parents now that the father is out of a job. There seems to be slightly more integration in both No. 31 and No. 46 because the children are assuming leadership and *they* are more adaptable than their parents. Perhaps we can generalize this process by saying that over a considerable period of time a family may make readjustments which its original structure could hardly achieve provided that the younger generation comes to share in the power.

The evidence regarding Type VI can be quickly summarized. Being poorly integrated originally, the decrease cannot harm them much, while their moderate adaptability gives them some readjustive power. A change under these circumstances is likely to be for the better, since even at this level the decrease is somewhat of a challenge.

CHAPTER XI

UNINTEGRATED, UNADAPTABLE FAMILIES

At last we have come to the very nether regions of our levels of family organization. And, fortunately for the world but unfortunately for this study, the representatives of Type VIII seem very scarce, at least among the families of college students. Only one such family was brought to the surface in our net. This case, No. 28, encountered a decrease with similar positions.

CASE NO. 28

The Lehmbruck family is descended from Austrian nobility and right here, perhaps, is the key to their situation. The whole family and Mr. Lehmbruck in particular have never forgotten this fact. At the time of the decrease he was 47, Mrs. Lehmbruck was 49, and their only child, Gretchen,* was 20. They lived in what had formerly been a lumbering section of northern Wisconsin. Their large 12-room house was on a sort of ranch three miles outside a small town. Here they had a three-car garage with large servant quarters over it, and a boathouse on a small lake containing canoes, rowboats, outboard motors, and one launch. Adjacent was a cement swimming pool. The home was lavishly furnished and a great deal of expensive entertaining was done for the wealthier families of the neighborhood. There were three servants.

Mr. Lehmbruck was a very high-strung, domineering man who carried on the tradition of such conduct among his rather unbalanced ancestors. He had an excellent physique and was energetic, with grandiose plans for the future. He was difficult in the home because of his ungovernable temper, but was charming to outsiders and well liked among his neighbors and associates. He had been in the lumber business, but when that had played out he had entered politics, serving several terms as state senator at Madison. His income amounted to $4000 a year or more, depending upon how successful he was in playing the stock market. He belonged to two fraternal organizations and several clubs in addition. His favorite recreations were hunting, fishing, and photography. He was very extravagant in his personal expenditures. He gambled a great deal and drank too much. Sometimes his temper got the better of him even in public, so that he alienated friends for short periods from time to time. The popularity of his wife probably helped him to maintain his friendships. He was jealous, however, of the attention shown his wife and daughter. When his daughter was at home he and she had bitter quarrels.

Mrs. Lehmbruck had not been in good health

for several years. Still, she appeared well and her cheerful and winning personality made her a pleasant companion. She was a splendid mixer and a charming hostess. Her greatest desire was to see her daughter well started in life, either married or in a successful business career. She was sincere and had the habit of keeping her troubles with her husband to herself. She was much more economical than her husband despite the fact that the income derived from her inherited property amounted to $4000 a year. She liked to have her daughter's friends in the home and frequently entertained for them. She was a member of the Eastern Star, a worker for the Red Cross, chairman of a local welfare committee and an interested political campaigner. Before her health made it impossible, she had been quite athletic, riding and playing tennis. She had a hobby of collecting sea shells, which yearly winter trips to Florida had enabled her to pursue.

Gretchen was an energetic girl interested in three types of activity—sports, parties, and music. She played tennis, golf and badminton, swam well and rode horseback a great deal. She was accomplished on both the piano and violin. But above all she liked to dance and play around with her "crowd" of boys and girls. She was well liked by this group though her temper sometimes offended them. She was very moody—usually gay, but occasionally sad. In general she did not take matters

225

very seriously and lived a rather superficial existence. She was a sophomore in college at the time
of the decrease. Her academic work was fairly
good, but she was not particularly conscientious
about it. She was working on the staff of one of
the publications and was in other activities. Her
mother did not let her join a sorority but she was
active in the dormitory in which she lived. She
was somewhat spoiled as a child with the result
that she had a jealous nature which showed itself
when others were preferred to her by some one
she liked. She was trying with some success to
control the manifestation of this, but she continued to feel it as much as ever. She was intending at this time to become a lawyer. She had a
liberal allowance from her mother.

All the members of the family shared the father's pride in its lineage and the idea that they
were aristocrats was very firmly rooted. They
were admittedly snobbish toward those they considered their social inferiors. The daughter had
been forced to change these ideas to a considerable extent after her entrance to college, but it was
a wrench for her to do so.

The leadership in the family belonged entirely
to the mother. There was a pretense by Mr. Lehmbruck that he was the real head, but the mother
"was the actual boss." The mother and daughter
really clung together in more or less opposition to
the father. He was, in their eyes, a rather ridic-

ulous figure. He was always dissatisfied about something, frequently about his alleged lack of clothes. He had in fact an extensive wardrobe, one far beyond any possible needs. He tried to pose as a martinet in the household because he believed that was the proper role for the head of a noble family.

All members of the family seemed to be rather two-faced. "At one moment they would be charming, and at the next glare at one as though capable of murder." Threats of suicide as a weapon against other members were frequently used. The mother and daughter constantly nagged Mr. Lehmbruck about his excessive drinking. Gretchen had deliberately become intoxicated once or twice to shame her father, but without effect. He was similarly nagged about his smoking, for he had developed a bad cough from it. However, the family waters ran smoother when Gretchen was away, for she was more critical in these matters than her mother.

The family prior to the decrease had very material standards. Mr. Lehmbruck's chief aim in life was to get and spend as much money as possible.

Despite the internal bickerings the family members did some things together. They often rode together and once or twice a year they visited Chicago as a family. However, when Gretchen was home it was rare for them all to be at dinner together. Actually they saw very little of one another. There was no church attendance and there was no emphasis on religion in the home, in spite of the fact that both the mother and father had been strictly brought up in this regard.

The family did draw together however, whenever a member was threatened from without, as when the daughter was in a bad automobile accident. Her father could not do enough to clear her of any guilt and, surprisingly, he did not upbraid her afterward. The fact was that there was no discipline to speak of, with the result that Gretchen encountered trouble when she entered the University. But she still thought she could have her own way. "When she was a little girl of 5 years she was the boss of a neighborhood gang in Chicago. Of course they lived on the select North Side, so she associated with only the best children. However, she would bribe the children to do as she wished, if they wouldn't obey her otherwise, by giving them candy."

The Lehmbrucks had sent Gretchen to an expensive boarding school but had shown no interest in her academic progress. "When she was home from school their main interests were in giving parties in her honor and seeing that she was properly entertained every minute of her visit. Her home did not seem like a home at all but more like a hotel where she was a non-paying guest."

The decrease came with Mr. Lehmbruck's loss

of political office and the decline in security values. He is at present doing nothing remunerative, though he still has a small income from investments. He seems to be in good health but will not be so long if he keeps up his increased drinking. "If you attempt to make him stop this excessive drinking he deliberately drinks more because he does not like to be told what he should do. He no longer has any plans for the future and all the ambition that he had before has vanished into thin air. He is still as selfish as ever, and is now economy mad." He tries to stop all family expenditures except those which he enjoys. "He has shown his quarrelling nature to many since the depression. Whereas before he never let his friends know how ugly he could be, he now doesn't seem to care. Every so often he has to have a big fight with some one, no matter who or about what, so he can rave and roar and think that he is in the right. He has only one car now, but he still gambles extensively. He has shown a great deal more antagonism toward his daughter since this decrease in his income. There is no definite reason for this, but he is decidedly jealous of the attention shown to both her and his wife. He has lost a large number of friends lately on account of his ungovernable temper and it is only through kindness and respect for his wife that some of his former friends tolerate him at all."

Mrs. Lehmbruck seems to be in better health

than she has been for some years. She has only one servant now so that she spends much more time on housework than she used to. She still entertains a good deal, and on almost as lavish a scale as formerly. The family had to resign from the country club, however, and this was a severe blow to her vanity. She has had to abandon the regular winter trip to Florida. Her income from her mother's estate is greatly reduced. Her friends are the same as before, and many of them are also suffering from financial reverses. She is having more difficulty than ever with her husband and a divorce would seem very likely were it not that both he and she consider a divorce a disgrace.

Gretchen has been in poor health since the decrease and will have to leave college shortly to undergo an operation. This makes her feel that she is a considerable drag on the family purse. She has continued her interest in sports as much as her health would permit. Her social affairs have been somewhat curtailed because of the reduction in her allowance. She still, however, has a car of her own. She has dropped her musical interests, but her interest in other worth-while concerns has increased, particularly her college studies. She is strongly considering marrying in the near future.

The decrease has reduced a little the snobbishness of the family and this has reacted to win them friendships among people who were formerly antagonistic.

Internally there is a paradoxical situation. There is more quarrelling and at the same time more cohesion. They feel the threat of the decrease and the need for a united front but at the same time the attempts to cut down expenses bring about bitter conflicts. The mother and daughter try to include the father in their plans more than they did, and he in his turn shows more interest in his daughter.

The three see more of each other because they cannot afford to have so many meals away from home. There is also some evidence that the mother and daughter are getting a new set of values and realizing that they formerly had too materialistic standards.

The Lehmbrucks illustrate again the formless character of unintegrated families. A new factor like a decrease in income must certainly be regarded as influential in the group life, and yet the utter lack of structure makes the character of the influence very difficult to describe or define. Unless one has a set of co-ordinates, a framework of some kind, one cannot plot changed relations. The fact that this family did not fare very well even when confronted with merely a simple decrease leads us to expect that the stronger pressures of modified and changed positions would play havoc with families of this type.

CHAPTER XII

SPECIAL FEATURES AND PROBLEMS

WHEN one has studied a mass of data from a certain point of view and with a particular set of concepts, one feels at the end that a great deal of good material has been wasted because the particular approach used has not exhausted the possibilities for analysis. In the present instance I am fully aware that there is present in these family case histories material which would repay investigation from other angles than that from which I have approached them. I have, however, no intention—at least at this time—of undertaking any such analysis, and will therefore defer to my dislike of waste only to the extent of examining briefly a few of the other features and problems which stood out as I was pursuing the main line of my investigation. Unfortunately there are not enough cases concerned in most of the matters I shall discuss to warrant making any but the most tentative generalizations.

The three-generations household is of considerable sociological interest because of the possibilities of conflicting cultures and of all those problems suggested by "mother-in-law jokes." In our cases there are six such families—Numbers 3, 4,

5, 16, 18, 35—in three of which the maternal grandmother lived in the household, in two of which it was the paternal grandfather, and in one the paternal grandmother.

So far as our evidence goes, the maternal grandmother seems to fit into the household satisfactorily. This is perhaps because the wife is home much more than her husband and is naturally more congenial with her own mother than she would be with her husband's. The one case in which this did not prove wholly true was No. 3, which was used as an example of Type V in Chapter II. In this instance one of the sources of friction was the grandmother's favoritism for the one grandchild that had lived with her as a baby. Also her attempts to help with the housework were often hindrances to her daughter who wanted to do things her own way. After the decrease there was less friction, though whether this could be laid to that fact is problematical, since the grandmother's increasing age and inability to be as active in the family life as before had much to do with it. In Case No. 5 one might have expected to find friction because the grandmother was "still living in the '90's." Such was not the fact, however, because the whole family was impressed with its rather aristocratic English lineage and the grandmother served as a perfect symbol of this.

The single case in which there was a paternal grandmother in the household, No. 35, shows a less harmonious situation. Here the mother, to quote, "resented deeply the dependent mother-in-law. Felt as if she were her 'cross' to bear. Not jealous, but just resented having her about. Thought mother-in-law tried to 'boss' her. They were not the same kind of housekeepers. Mother wanted to run her own house the way she wanted to." The mother-in-law resented her daughter-in-law's attitude toward her and felt out of place in her son's home. She hated to be dependent and was unhappy over the situation. She tried hard not to be in the way, but she wanted to go places with the family and didn't seem to realize that her son and his wife would like to go alone occasionally. After the decrease the mother was thrown with the grandmother more, but on the other hand they seemed to come to a better understanding; so that if anything the friction decreased.

There was no friction in either of the cases involving the paternal grandfather, No. 16 and No. 18. In the former, to quote, "I do not believe there is any reason for including him (in this analysis) because he has very little intercourse with the family. By choice he cooks his own meals, has his own room, and because he is entirely deaf, really lives apart from the family life. Since he is 85 years old, he is quite feeble and is hardly interested in the family problems, in fact, not aware of them. He is self-supporting also, so he does not offer any financial burden or problem. As a factor in the family life, he neither affects nor is affected by any change in the financial condition." The other case, No. 18, is that of a jolly, though rather individualistic family, in which the grandfather, a 70-year-old printer, was at the time of the decrease steadily employed in a shop which he half owned. He was "a kindly old man of wonderful health and energy . . . easy-going in temperament but not a man to be trod on . . . always cheerful and optimistic . . . willing at all times to give up part of his share to those unluckier than he, sympathetic and understanding, greatly in love with his son and daughter-in-law and his grandsons . . . generous and open-handed to a fault." He went his own way a good deal of the time and had his own friends, but he never failed to accommodate himself to the rest of the family. His failure to be thrifty caused him remorse when the decrease came and he could not help the family very much. However, the depression knitted this individualistic family considerably closer.

Another problem of somewhat the same type is that of step-parents and stepchildren. Only three of our families involved such relationships. Of these only one, No. 13, contained two sets of children, and this case we have discussed rather completely in Chapter III. In this instance, it may be recalled, the family was well enough integrated and sufficiently adaptable to prove invulnerable to a decrease with similar positions. One of the other

235

cases, No. 15, contained a stepmother whom the father had married after the children were grown. The situation here was well indicated by the fact that the girl who was writing the case did not include the stepmother in her first draft analysis. When I called this to her attention, she wrote: "The mother came into the family at the peak of the family fortunes. She was a quiet sort of person and really entered very little into the life of the family. She took more the place of a housekeeper than a mother. Although there was some friction in regard to money matters . . . the final settlement . . . went to the father who settled them with great tact so that it seemed to cause no appearance of favoritism. The fact that the mother was a stepmother really didn't create much friction. The family had been used to rather inquisitive housekeepers, and she was hardly more than this, and, being a rather negative character, her existence in the family was not a problem. The children were happy that their father had found a congenial companion and really strove to ease the situation for him." After the decrease it is stated: "The mother has become more deeply entrenched in the life of the family, and it has become increasingly apparent to the children that she has made the father much happier. Relations between the mother and children are on the whole amiable, with only superficial disagreements."

The last step-relation case, No. 8, presents, before the decrease, the interesting situation of father, stepmother and only child, a boy, with the father away at least half the year as an engineer on a lake freighter, and the stepmother and stepchild making their home together. In this instance the boy remembered his own mother, who died when he was 7, and he had not become attached to his foster mother, who entered the household 3 years later. The situation was an extremely individualistic one, since the father was away so much and the two at home were not congenial. Even when the father was home he was quiet and retiring and did not make himself intimate with his child. The decrease in income brought the father back into the home, for he took a position as a stationary engineer on shore. This made for more family feeling and more common activity. In addition the stepmother's health failed, and the ensuing sorrow of the husband and stepchild at her dependence was undoubtedly an integrating factor. Finally, this meant the end of her tendency to dominate the boy. The father's return gives the modification of position here a definitely integrating effect and makes this case a difficult one to classify. Perhaps it should have been excluded as not being a typical family situation originally.

Before leaving the consideration of unusual original family situations it might be interesting to examine Case No. 9. Here we see the unwillingness of a family to let a "black sheep" break the group unity. Let me quote: "Even when my brother got in trouble, which was often, my mother would never let any one else (outside the family) criticize him, even though she gave him good bawlings out. Dad always forgave and hoped for better things in the future. . . . My older brother has the faculty of making friends, and secured business for dad. The only thing about him was that he trailed with a lot of good-for-nothings who could not pay (hence dad got stung) and who got him into trouble, keeping dad in constant hot water. I know of many customers dad lost because W. K.'s name was in the paper for being drunk, so, while W. K. meant to help by getting orders, he was really hindering all the time. W. K. was married and did not live with us. Dad and mother both did all they possibly could to help him—to develop him. He is a likable enough fellow but can't stay away from women and drink. The folks got him started in housekeeping, dad took him into the office and gave him every opportunity to learn the business. They saw him through two divorces from the same woman. All this time the folks helped him financially. Upon being married a third time, this time to a different woman, the folks again set him up in housekeeping, but again he did not do well. . . . My dad and mother have offered him every advantage only to be disappointed every time in him. Still they cling to him, trying to change his attitude, but to no avail. Father lent him money, mother helped his wife, bought clothes for his wife and even sacrificed her own clothes for his wife's needs, dad raised his salary and gave him $50 a week for his duties that were not worth $30 the way he attended to them." Nor do the younger brothers criticize their parents for their attempts to straighten out their elder. The whole family feels keenly the necessity of pulling together and even the erring brother is in many ways a loyal family member.

Case No. 47 makes an arresting human interest story, though its contributions from a scientific standpoint are doubtful because of the uncertainty as to just what part the decrease in income played in the turn events took. The family was Ukrainian in origin and was closely integrated in an active Ukrainian colony in Cleveland. On festival days the family members wore the national costume and there were frequent picnics and other gatherings of the folk. There were three children—a girl of 19, a boy of 13, and a baby. The father was a successful and optimistic window cleaner who had established himself in American life and hoped to do better. The mother worked irregularly in a restaurant. The girl, beside doing much of the housework, had entered a local college just before the decrease came. She had persuaded her parents to let her try college, though they doubted her ability to do the work because her high-school marks had not been good. She, however, felt that was because of the time devoted to household duties. Though not bright, she was attractive and had many friends. She was hoping to marry a particular man, who was well educated and of higher economic status. Some of her other boy friends were of questionable character.

When the decrease came by reason of the father's dwindling employment and the mother's loss of her job, the daughter had to leave college. The family was shortly reduced to a starvation diet and were soon suffering from malnutrition. About the same time, the girl's hope in the way of marriage died because the man married another girl. This, on top of her inability to continue her education, embittered her to the degree that she became seclusive. She would go nowhere, using as an excuse that her clothes were too shabby. It was under these circumstances that she came under the influence of a married relative who seduced her. Upon the discovery of their repeated illicit relations, the man's wife left him and there was a family scandal. The girl was severely criticized by her parents and she decided to leave home. At this juncture another man offered to take her to New York as his mistress, and she accepted, knowing that the relation would probably not last, and intending to become a prostitute when he left her. When her family discovered where she was, they implored her to return, and this she finally did.

The upshot of the situation is a strained and unhappy family, existing on miserable food, the mother sick with gallstones and her health otherwise impaired, the father without hope, the daughter sullen and discontented and almost friendless. The fine solidarity that there was before is replaced by indifference to one another that amounts almost to distrust. Though it is against their principles, they expect to be forced on "the welfare" soon.

The last direction on the family analysis blank was as follows: "You have discussed the family situation before the decrease in income and after it had its effect. Now use this sheet and as many more as you need to describe what the process of change was." As this study has been organized, there has been no opportunity to consider this process. It might be of interest therefore to quote one of the more complete and at the same time fairly typical answers to this question. Case No. 1 fulfills these requirements.

This case has been classified as belonging to Type I and as suffering a decrease with similar positions. It therefore withstood the pressure well. The original situation was in brief this: The father was in the real-estate business in a city of more than 100,000. His income was about $8000 a year. He was a hard worker, kind to his family, a pillar of the church, and had many friends. The

mother was of a similar type, cheerful, lenient with
her children, doing her housework and helping out
at the office. Laura, age 24, was a school-teacher
in the city. She was generous with her money and
helped her mother at home, though she did not
have a strong family sense and was inclined to
keep to herself. She had few friends. Fredericka,
21, was a stenographer and a quite different sort
from her sister. She "dated" frequently, saved little, and helped very little at home. Arthur, 20, was
in the University. His hobby was sailing. He was
a normal young man, mingled with friends of
both sexes and was careful in his expenditures.
The oldest daughter, Frances, was married and
putting her husband through medical school by
teaching music. There was a good deal of family
pride and solidarity. Such was the situation prior
to the decrease.

"The first development was a very much short-
ened vacation for all of us last summer (1930).
All had plans for the fall and we did not think
much about it. We were willing to shorten our
vacation and work longer that summer. Father
had not made a single deal all summer. The apartments were not renting and vacancies cut down the
income almost entirely. The position of Frances
allowed her to continue putting her husband
through his last year of medicine without needing
aid from home. Fredericka had her position for 3
months after school began. When she was let out

of work all co-operated in trying to find work for her, but to no avail. Fredericka was not co-operating to the full extent. Perhaps she is the most selfish and Frances comes next in spite of the fact that she put her husband through medicine. It is known that she considered it as a good investment. This was not entirely due to selfishness, but was stressed by the husband in order to encourage her. It was not a great sacrifice until the months of April and May during her developed pregnancy. Fredericka . . . had all her time unoccupied but aided mother only occasionally with the housework. This can be explained by her social inclinations. She was going with her future husband and since her aims were worthy and she was successful, she might be excused from too severe a criticism. The sympathetic discipline continued and perhaps it is mother's kind-heartedness which kept Fredericka from realizing her partial negligence. Arthur, with his $200 a year income and with his savings from the 1930 summer, put himself through the first two months of school, including tuition, books and fraternity dues. When his savings were gone, Laura loaned $30 to $50 a month for his use. Her $2200 a year enabled her to do this as well as pay a small fee to her parents for room and board. During the year she loaned her father $100-$150 besides. Laura is small and frail and this is the reason for her not helping very much with housework.

"Christmas, 1930, shows a marked change in family routine. Each of the children bought a present for both mother and father. Among the children we drew names so that each younger person had to buy only one gift for another younger person. Thus each of the younger persons bought three gifts; one for father, one for mother, and one for one of the younger persons. Father and mother were prohibited from buying any gifts except for each other and for outside friends whom they had to remember. Thus our Christmas was for our parents mostly, and they certainly deserved it and much more.

"Following Christmas the tension grew steadily greater. Fredericka was always willing to get work, but then began definitely to look for work but without success. Laura was generous throughout but by now she ceased golf (except with boy friends) and refrained from buying unnecessary but desirable objects, such as odd teapots, beautiful linens, etc., offered at a very attractive price. This was a great sacrifice for Laura because she has a passion for dainty things and she always keeps them well and finds a use for them.

"By April father had made one deal. Arthur looked for a board job at school but only succeeded in picking up odd jobs and substituting for waiters or dishwashers, usually over a week-end. Arthur went home week-ends after May in order to save board money and also in order to canvass his home town for prospective campers at the camp in which he is going to work this summer. Each camper would bring him $15 commission. As yet he has been unsuccessful in this work because the camp fee is high and most people are looking for work rather than a vacation.

"The tension became greater after April. Between April and June father made three deals but they were scarcely noticed among the floating debts that demanded money and were often overdue. We all became more sympathetic. We were all told to look for work, but there was little impatience if we did not find work, because we all realize how scarce work is. Father's worry has been very great throughout and could hardly become any greater. We all cheer each other as much as possible, but there is little we can do except continue our diplomacy. This increase in diplomacy has been very marked and shows how intelligence or education is an actual and vital aid in meeting crises. We have co-operated in continuing the development of one another.

"This summer (1931) brings Laura's teaching to a close and she has not yet found work. The summer of 1930 she worked in a department store and she would take almost anything offered now. Laura has gotten work for next winter. Fredericka is married and since her husband is a high salaried man her condition is greatly improved and the expenditure of the family is lightened somewhat. Arthur will be working at camp with all expenses paid but a very indefinite idea as to income, possibly $50-$200. Frances will, of course, be unable to work until very late summer at the earliest. If she finds work for next winter she will be doing her part. She has gone home three week-ends in order to look for a winter teaching position, but being married is a most serious handicap.

"Father has become cross. His mental activities show a slight lag although he has recently thought out very brilliant schemes for shifting property. The repeated failures would wear on any one's mind. Father has stood up well. His exercise at the Y. M. C. A. is a very wise routine. Father is the only one who can administer his property and he knows it. He has often told Arthur that the business dies with the 'old man.' That is why father wants Arthur to complete his education. Medicine is the choice and it will be commenced this fall if conditions enable. Mother is forcing herself to be bright and cheerful. It is somewhat forced now, but it is fundamentally inherent in her. . . . Mother and father are doing entirely too much work, but there is no one else who can help them with the business. A more severe administrator would turn out the renter and get more people in of a hard or 'tough' type. This type has always been distasteful to father and he does not allow late parties, at least in his furnished apartments. He is fairly broad-minded and it requires several repetitions or complaints to make father ask the people to move. One reason for father's crossness is the absolute patience which he needs during the day in his work. Most of our friends would not believe that father is ever cross . . . and it is only the let-down of home that allows the strain to show up in his crossness.

"It is hard to predict the future. It will be a matter of years before debts can all be paid off, for the normal income would not be sufficient to liquidate very rapidly. Deals are beginning to pick up but it will still be months before many people will again invest in property. The property has decreased in value at least 25 per cent and the assessments have not been lowered.

"Generalizations: The strain was greatly increased by the depression. It is felt by all, but is felt more by father and mother. Co-operation increased as well as family unity and 'we' feeling. Greater effort on the part of all, but the girls did not help with the housework as much as they could have. Scarcity of work is an added and *increasing* strain. All help with the development and advancement of each member of the family. The situation has encouraged the exercise of psychology by all, but to a minor degree in the case of Fredericka and father."

In our series there were three cases in which the

decrease made necessary, or at least was accompanied by, the change of residence of the family from one town to another. All three moved to Ann Arbor—No. 10 from Saginaw, No. 50 from California, and No. 52 from Royal Oak, Michigan. Both No. 10 and No. 52 have been discussed previously, the former in Chapter VIII, the latter in Chapter VII. A rereading of these two cases will indicate that the transition was not without its hardships, for in both cases parents who had been closely integrated into community life found themselves with almost no friends or connections in Ann Arbor. In each instance mention is made by the writer of the isolation of the mother particularly and her attempts to make up for her lack of contacts by increasing devotion to her family. In No. 10 there were student roomers also to take the mother's time and energy. Case No. 50 has not been previously discussed, but it shows the same thing. This was a Type I family that suffered a decrease with similar positions, and hence came through with flying colors. However, the shift from the former community was a wrench. Let me quote, first in regard to the original situation in California:

"The family had established itself as one of the upper middle-class, socially prominent, professional families. The parents belonged to and held offices in the leading city organizations and were whole-heartedly interested in civic affairs. One educational group met regularly twice a month at their home for 2 years. The family lived a great deal with other families, participating with them in picnics, and day trips to the beaches. . . . The family did not think of itself as 'we,' but as 'we all, families and everybody else belong to each other'—this is the spirit of the West."

After the decrease in income and the move to Ann Arbor: "This move was serious because it meant the loss of a permanent home and friends of years' standing. Entering the new city as strangers, hampered financially to make proper advances socially, the family was . . . depressed for over a year. They could not dress, entertain or enter into social or civic affairs as they had been accustomed to. They did not have the interest either, the Eastern atmosphere with its individualism not appealing to them as did the Western spirit. The mother in particular found it very difficult to arouse interest in resettling a new house and rebuilding a social life for the family. Mary particularly suffered for her old friends and the first 2 years wrote voluminous and frequent letters to them. The father did not mind the adjustment as much as the other members because he liked his new teaching position and his work went on uninterruptedly. . . . After 3 years in the new town the family has . . . really begun to build up its

social life again; but this time more casually—
the first fiery spark has gone."

Turning from the decrease itself to some of the
special situations which arise as a result of it, we
find several that are noteworthy. A number of
cases show a sequence of slight disorganization
followed by reorganization. One of these, Case
No. 15, was the one mentioned earlier in this chapter in which the stepmother was formerly regarded
as merely a housekeeper by her stepchildren. I
quote: "The first effects of the change on the
members of the family were of the more disinte-
grative nature, and, as the change showed more
evidence of being permanent, the mutual sympathies became aroused. The earlier cuts in luxuries tended to hit the children first, because they
spent more of this part of the family income than
did the parents. Consequently at first the reaction
of the younger members was rather unsympathetic
until they came more to understand the family
position and accommodated themselves to it. By a
gradual process the family has come to a greater
unity of understanding as to its situation."

It is interesting to inquire how this sequence of
events fits into our general theory. One might suppose that if a family were invulnerable to a certain type of pressure, there would be not even temporary disorganization. Yet it is explainable on
the ground that, though potentially capable of

meeting the impinging force, it takes time for the resistance to become organized, so that the family staggers, as it were, from the initial blow. There is another explanation, not proper to the case just cited, but suggested in the last sentence of Chapter X. Internal factors such as the growing up of children may modify the structure of the whole to a degree that the family, originally vulnerable to the particular pressure encountered, may, over a considerable period of time, readjust in such a way as to regain its lost solidarity. This would be a reorganization not entirely forced from without, but one in which both external and internal changes play a part. Very few of our cases cover a long enough time span for this process to appear.

In our theoretical scheme we have described the results, at least in the integrated cases, as either a maintenance or a breaking of the socio-psychological structure of family life. No account is taken of qualitative changes in the structure itself. We will examine two cases which are particularly interesting from this point of view.

Case No. 39 is concerned with a Type V family. They were German Jews of the intellectual type. Both grandfathers had been teachers in Europe. The father was a successful accountant with rather wordly standards, who was not intimate with his two sons. The mother pampered the older boy and was severe with the younger, causing friction. Both boys were cultured and well read. Unity was felt in terms of high economic status (income of $6000) and intellectual traditions.

The decrease with similar positions has had considerable effect in shifting the emphasis in the family unity. "The members now stay at home more than they usually did before the decrease, as now there is no money for very many outside activities. This has also helped to establish a better co-operative feeling. The family now shares its joys and sorrows with more feeling, as I have noticed on several occasions. Another thing that I have noticed is a greater feeling for religious custom and ritual. My father and mother now attend services regularly. At times I have even heard my father remark 'Thank God we are at least able to maintain a home together.' My mother too has remarked on several of my visits home, that she wishes I were through with school and living at home. . . . A solidarity of a new type has developed based on a simple emotion, rather than on any cultural or intellectual ideal, and on the loss of income. Or is this a rational compensation for the loss of other factors in our material life?"

Perhaps the oddest qualitative change in the family unity in our series is indicated in Case No. 26. Here we find a man of aristocratic lineage (a brother of Mr. Lehmbruck whose family was discussed in the last chapter) who had come down to the position of managing a country club with the help of his wife. There were two girls, aged at the time of the decrease 11 and 3. The father was a heavy drinker, rather quarrelsome, but withal likable. The mother, a former school-teacher, was bitter because her dreams of a fine life had been disappointed. She nagged her husband into working and stayed with him only for the sake of the children. The family kept up a good front and impressed the neighbors, but their income was only $3500. There was little system in the home, and the older girl was introverted and unhappy. The mother was often cruel to the children, perhaps as a compensation for her own suffering. I have classified the family as belonging to Type VI.

The decrease with similar positions brought about a regression of the mother to the level of the father. He has changed little except that he drinks more, the mother has abandoned her careful habits and seems to have adopted the principle of getting pleasure while you can. She spends more than formerly, though they can afford it much less, has become interested in rather lavish entertaining, has hired a maid and is about to get a second car in addition to the Packard they already own. All this has produced a greater harmony in the family, for the father and mother now see more or less eye-to-eye. One cannot but wonder what the ultimate outcome will be when the family credit is exhausted, but at least for the time being one cannot say that the feeble family structure has broken.

Rather it seems to have maintained itself by a sort of childish flight from reality.

We come finally to the extreme psychological effects of economic crisis on family members. In almost all the cases there are noticeable changes, but in five of them these are so strong as to amount almost to a mechanism of escape. It is interesting to note that in every instance it is the father and chief breadwinner who is thus affected. One may conclude either that, because he has always had the responsibility for the family's economic security, the loss of such security weighs more heavily upon him than upon any one else, or that the wife's household tasks are so preoccupying as to distract her in some degree from the family troubles.

These extreme effects show themselves in two fields, the religious and the politico-economic. Two cases, No. 14 and No. 24, exemplify the first situation; two, No. 11 and No. 47, the second; and one, No. 30, both.

Case No. 14 was dealt with at some length in Chapter V. It will be recalled as that of the Klein family in which the father had a sort of mental breakdown, one result of which was the development of a creed of self-expression and of a corresponding indifference toward Judaism. Formerly he had been a devout participant. This defection became a point of difficulty with the rest of the family, and in particular with Mrs. Klein. The same sort of break in fundamental orientation occurred in Case No. 24. Here we find a good-natured, hard-working, wholesome farmer, who had been regular in church attendance, though not particularly devout, turning, after the decrease, to a spiritualistic cult. Let us quote: "His cheerful nature has become a disgruntled nature. He broods and worries over everything conceivable—and some things that are inconceivable. It isn't a case of his resenting the fact that he and the family have to do without, but it is a case of worrying lest the condition get so bad that the family security would be threatened. Of course there is no *reason* for such an attitude because the family has adjusted its expenditures to the cut in income *very* successfully. This change is reflected in his increased activity—he works more and has less leisure. In what little leisure he has he seems to prefer to be alone more than he did formerly. He has found a partial escape from his pessimism in a spiritualistic cult to which he has been all but actually converted—a thing to which he would never have attached any significance formerly. The other members of the family ridicule his new 'fanaticism' freely and abusively." Speaking of the change in the mother the writer says: "There are some rather serious quarrels between her and her husband over his newly acquired spiritualism. It embarrasses her greatly to have to admit that she is powerless to prevent the matter." And later: "It embarrasses the family in social and church relations and besides is making the father rather 'queer.' He resents the ridicule but does not retort. However, when his wife tries to prevent his going [to the spiritualist meetings] by arranging for some other use of the car he 'blows up.' He feels that he has an inalienable right to *some* 'freedom.' "

The symptoms of personal maladjustment do not always take the form merely of rebellion against generalized schemes of life orientation. They also take the form of rebellion against the political and economic system itself. As would be expected those showing this reaction are on lower rungs of the economic ladder and have suffered its injustices. The father in Case No. 11 was an intelligent, self-educated factory hand who was born in Ontario but had lived in Michigan ever since his marriage in 1897. Before the depression he was not in the least radical, though mildly liberal. "I had never heard of him speaking against the wealthy classes until the last couple of years and at times he gets real bitter against them. . . . He will listen to political speeches for a while, then shut the radio off and argue against the speaker." He "is no longer his old, energetic self. This is (partly) due to pessimism against the economic system in general."

We find the same result in Case No. 47, the Ukrainian family which was discussed earlier in this chapter. It will be recalled that the father was a window washer, who, until the depression, had hopes of rising to a higher position in American life. Now "his attitude toward life is . . . pessimistic; to him everything seems to go wrong and every capitalist is detrimental to the welfare of humanity and the capitalist system absolutely stands on a rotten foundation. Moreover, he thinks there is no cure for the present depression; the capitalists have the nation's wealth and will not 'play fair' with the poor people unless through a revolution they are forced to play otherwise. As to recovery from this depression he is hopeless; as to a radical change which is bound to come, he is optimistic."

Case No. 30 illustrates change in both religious and economic thought. The family is Jewish and of Russian heritage, though the father was born in England and the mother in this country. Before the depression the father, a travelling salesman, is described as orthodox in religion to the point of superstition, a 100 per cent patriot, and a rugged individualist of the do-others-before-they-do-you variety. Since the decrease "he has become less religious, tending now toward agnosticism but retaining all his sympathies for the race of his forefathers." In regard to the economic system "his philosophy has become more radical but his actions in the commercial world have not changed."

CHAPTER XIII

RETROSPECT AND SYNTHESIS

THE time has come to draw away from the trees far enough to see the woods. We have been so occupied with the study of the details of our problem that we must again take our stand, as at the beginning, in a position from which a panoramic view may be obtained. What, then, have we done and learned?

The problem with which we started was to discover types of family life on the socio-psychological level which would show specific reactions to a severe decrease in income from accustomed sources. We soon discovered that such a decrease was not a simple thing and that different degrees of pressure had to be recognized. This required that changes on the symbiotic or sustenance level of family life which accompanied the decrease should be included as part of the pressure. The complication thus introduced made our problem the more difficult one of discovering family types which would show characteristic reactions to three sets of conditions—a simple decrease, a decrease with modified positions on the symbiotic level, and a decrease with changed positions on that level. Analysis of 50 suitable families indicated that the

258

factors to be used in making up such types were integration and adaptability. Three degrees of each were distinguished, so that the nine possible combinations would theoretically produce nine types. Actually we discovered only eight of them in our series and therefore used only that number in the study. The one not appearing was that of unintegrated, highly adaptable families. On logical grounds we should expect such families to be very rare, if existent at all.

These eight types are not "cultural" types, as the anthropologist uses that term. Although there were different heritages represented in the families studied, the differentiation employed was not in any way comparable to such a division as one into Irish, old American, Polish, and German families. The types do not represent heritage at all, but rather actual family relations and potential family process. The differences in these respects were thought of as all occurring within the American stream of culture. There is no obvious reason why our types would not also be found occurring in other cultures, though one should certainly not assert that they do without investigation. Even if they did, the considerations which enter into the judgment of the degree of adaptability or of integration might be quite different. We have stated in considerable detail the actual reactions of the various types to the three pressures wherever we had cases as evidence, and the probable reactions where that could be inferred by comparison and crude interpolation or extrapolation. The diagram on the following page gives a rough summary of the generalizations made throughout the several chapters with respect to these matters. The term "conflicting evidence" signifies that some of the families of the type in question when faced with the particular pressure indicated proved vulnerable, while others appeared invulnerable. This pressure may then be regarded as the critical pressure for that type. The single word "yielding" perhaps is an insufficient term for what happens to Type VI and Type VII families, for it will be recalled that there was often a sort of groping struggle for organization as well as the characteristic lack of resistance to pressure.

An examination of the diagram shows that, as we have previously suggested, there are great similarities in reaction of some of the types. One would really be losing very little in accuracy of analysis if one combined Types I and IV, II and V, III and VI, and VII and VIII. Then we would have four types which would be summarized as follows:

A. Integrated, highly adaptable families which are invulnerable to any sort of decrease.

B. Integrated, moderately adaptable families which are vulnerable to a changed-positions decrease and may sometimes be vulnerable to a modified-positions decrease.

REACTIONS OF FAMILY TYPES TO DIFFERENT DEGREES OF PRESSURE ASSOCIATED WITH DECREASE IN INCOME FROM ACCUSTOMED SOURCES

FAMILY TYPES	DEGREES OF PRESSURE		
	SIMILAR POSITIONS	MODIFIED POSITIONS	CHANGED POSITIONS
I. Highly Integrated, Highly Adaptable	Firmly Invulnerable	Readjustively Invulnerable	Readjustively Invulnerable
II. Highly Integrated, Moderately Adaptable	Firmly Invulnerable	Conflicting Evidence	Vulnerable
III. Highly Integrated, Unadaptable	Vulnerable	Vulnerable	Vulnerable
IV. Moderately Integrated, Highly Adaptable	Firmly Invulnerable	Readjustively Invulnerable	Readjustively Invulnerable
V. Moderately Integrated, Moderately Adaptable	Firmly Invulnerable	Readjustively Invulnerable	Vulnerable
VI. Moderately Integrated, Unadaptable	Conflicting Evidence	Vulnerable	Vulnerable
VII. Unintegrated, Moderately Adaptable	Yielding	Yielding	Yielding
VIII. Unintegrated, Unadaptable	Yielding	Yielding	Yielding

C. Integrated, unadaptable families which are vulnerable to any sort of decrease.

D. Unintegrated families which have not sufficient structure to resist pressure at all, but yield to it in unpredictable ways.

A scheme of this sort has the advantage of simplicity, but it blurs over some of the interesting differences of detail which seem to be present in the types combined above. For instance, Type I families are more similar to one another than Type IV families. This is because a highly integrated family can hardly vary much from an ideal pattern. The deficiencies which are present in Type IV families, however, may be of several kinds, such as cliques, individualism, or separation between the generations. There is the further difference that Type IV families, because they are further from the ideal, can mend their ways more spectacularly than Type I families as their latent powers are called out by the challenge of the depression.

Just as in the case of integration, the families in the more highly adaptable types tend to be more similar than those in the less highly adaptable. Perhaps this is even more true here, since the variety of deficiencies in adaptability is even greater than in integration.

A point not made apparent in the diagram, but which seems probable from the evidence, is that the relative significance of integration and adaptability shifts with the impingement of different pressures. For a simple decrease, integration is of considerable significance; while for a decrease with modified or changed positions adaptability becomes of overwhelming importance. This, after all, is common sense, since these are the situations which call for readjustment of roles and hence for family flexibility.

The matter of internal growth, referred to briefly in Chapter III, perhaps deserves further comment. It is quite conceivable that families would change their types over a period of time as the children grow up, especially if the younger generation is quite unlike the older. This fact has no doubt upset our analysis in one or two instances and may account for families meeting a decrease better than we would have expected, when the children are more adaptable than their parents. For example, by the time the depression has had its full effect the family may have shifted from Type III to Type II, and thus be invulnerable to a simple decrease when the condition of the family at the time of the decrease would have led us to expect that it would prove vulnerable.

Apart from such internal growth, the theory upon which this study rests assumes that only families which prove vulnerable to the decrease or yield to it are likely to change in type as a result of this experience with depression. The others, because successful, will not be stimulated to alter their character. Even where unsuspected latent powers have been called into play, the theory would be that no lasting modification in structure has occurred. This is a point of view which may well raise doubts and which deserves further study. Unfortunately the material gathered in this investigation does not provide the basis for either proof or disproof of the theory.

Many persons will wish that we could conclude with some positive statements as to what proportion of all families suffering a severe decrease in income survived the ordeal. Unfortunately such statements cannot be made. As explained in Chapter I, our series of cases is not in any sense a representative sample, even of the families of college students. The fact that most of these families came through with flying colors proves nothing whatever about the more general situation. This is not to say that this investigation might not prove helpful in answering the question. If one were now to secure a large and representative sample of American families, and if one classified them into the types here described, one would be able to make a fairly reliable prediction as to what percentage of them would be likely satisfactorily to meet stated situations of decreased income. Thus our study has done no more than to lay a modest foundation stone for others to build upon.

APPENDIX ON METHOD

SINCE the fact is that this whole study was undertaken to test some notions about research method in sociology rather than because of special interest in the family, it seems appropriate to treat methodological matters in some detail. The discussion is appended to the body of the text instead of being incorporated in it because readers who are interested in the substantive results may care little for methodology, while social scientists may be in the converse position. It is hoped that what is to follow will be a contribution in two directions: first, as a case study in the evolution of research method, indicating the tentative character of the procedure; and, second, as a modest critique of sociological method in general.

The mental "set" out of which the investigation grew is set forth in a "Memorandum Concerning a Proposed Research Technique" written in 1931.[1] I shall quote from it at some length.

"This memorandum is based upon the conception of social phenomena and social research so ably expressed by the late Charles H. Cooley . . . . It will be assumed that . . . the sociologist . . . must get at many of his data by 'sympathetic in-

[1] *Social Forces*, X, pp. 204-8.

sight.' This means . . . the use of the case method in one of its numerous forms.

"Assuming . . . that we wish to obtain valid generalizations of an analytic type . . . we must develop techniques of handling large numbers of case records comparatively. . . . One of the most obvious modes of attacking the problem . . . is to eliminate as many variables as possible at the outset by the way in which the problem is defined. . . . The entities selected for study should be fairly homogeneous. We may choose to investigate wives of professional men, boys' gangs, or rural churches. Further, it would seem desirable at the beginning not to deal with all the adjustments which these entities make to their environing situations, but to single out one condition which impinges upon all the entities of a given class and investigate their several adjustments to that condition. Thus we might try to discover how rural churches have adjusted to the coming of the automobile, how boys from immigrant families are affected by going to college, or how families with young children in which the father dies readjust following his death.

"There have been two ways by which this problem has been chiefly attacked. One is exemplified by Thomas and Znaniecki in the *Polish Peasant*. . . . The authors became very familiar with the case materials and then allowed their minds to winnow the wheat from the chaff so as to bring forth what seemed to be basic causal relationships. . . . A second approach has been by statistical procedures as exemplified by Burgess, Glueck and Vold in their studies of factors associated with parole violation.[1] . . . Indices are obtained by which one may predict the likelihood of an individual's success or failure on parole. This likelihood has to be stated in terms such as this: 20 per cent of the men who fall in the same index group as this individual have violated their parole. . . . This may be very valuable information for administrative purposes . . . but it certainly tells us very little about the fundamental factors which produce violation or non-violation. We would wish to know why 80 per cent followed one course while 20 per cent followed another.

"It is the aim of the memorandum to suggest that a more analytic use of statistics would be of great assistance in indicating where common causal relations lie embedded in large numbers of cases. . . . The ultimate aim is to secure generalizations which state that when a specified type of entity encounters a specified new condition, it adjusts in a specified way.

"We would begin, then, by securing case records

[1] E. W. Burgess, "Factors Determining Success or Failure on Parole," in Bruce, Harno, and Burgess, *Parole and the Indeterminate Sentence,* pp. 205–69; Sheldon Glueck and Elinor T. Glueck, "Predictability in the Administration of Criminal Justice," *Harvard Law Review,* XLII, 300–29; G. B. Vold, "Factors Entering into the Success or Failure of Minnesota Men on Parole, *Publications of the American Sociological Society,* XXIV, 167–73.

showing the characteristics of homogeneous entities prior to the impingement of a common new condition and their several adjustments to that condition. . . . We could then distribute the cases into a small number of adjustment classes according to the manner in which they have reacted to the new condition. The investigator, after going through these records carefully, will have certain 'hunches' as to what aspects of the entities evidenced previous to the impingement of the new condition were of significance in producing the subsequent adjustments. . . . Once a set of aspects has been determined upon, a few qualitative, or in some cases quantitative, characterizations would have to be decided upon in each aspect, so that each case would receive as many characterizations as there were aspects. . . . The things that require to be related, then, are these characterizations (as before the impingement) and the adjustments (subsequent thereto). And it is here that statistical procedures will enable us to carry forward a more complicated analysis than the human mind could possibly achieve unaided."

There followed in the memorandum a detailed discussion of just how this statistical analysis could be accomplished with the aid of punched cards and sorting and tabulating machines. The idea was to secure coefficients of contingency between combinations of characterizations and adjustment classes instead of between merely the characterizations in each aspect separately and these classes. It was thought this would preserve the "wholeness" of the cases instead of mutilating them to the extent that ordinary statistical analysis does. The suggestion was made that the investigator should return to case analysis once he had done his statistical work in order to "try to discover just how and why the characteristics associated with particular adjustments came to produce these results. It would of course be necessary to see why the misfits which would be present even in the table having the highest coefficient of contingency did not conform to the general trend. Thus we would be refining the analysis still further with the hope ultimately of getting at generalizations of the natural science kind."

When I came to choose a suitable project for the trying out of this proposed technique, I gave considerable thought to the possibilities of investigating the effects of entering college on various types of students. However, the family project was preferred on two grounds: first, because I believed the impinging force would be more nearly the same in different cases (a supposition which appears much more doubtful now that I have investigated families) and, second, because it seemed as if other impinging influences would be easier to rule out than in the case of students coming to a university.

Once decided on a field for investigation, I tried

to define the problem more rigorously so as to avoid waste of time and energy on irrelevancies. This process led to the ultimate adoption of the limitations discussed in Chapter I; to wit, (1) American families, (2) suffering a decrease in real income from accustomed sources of at least 25 per cent, (3) composed at the time of the decrease of parents and children living together, (4) in which the decrease was apparently lasting, (5) upon which it had come suddenly, and (6) in which no crucial event unconnected with the depression had occurred since the decrease. It was thought that these qualifications would select a relatively homogeneous set of families that had suffered a very similar pressure, the adjustment to which would be observable because of the suddenness of the decrease, its apparent persistence, and the precautions against the introduction of complicating factors.

It is of course obvious that there needed to be no effort to obtain a representative sample of any kind. I was not trying to get at averages of any kind, but to discover distinctive types having specific reactions to a decrease in income from accustomed sources.

Excerpts from two letters written in March and April, 1931, and addressed to the Committee on the Faculty Research Fund asking for a grant to conduct the study are revealing: "I expect . . . 40 to 50 good case histories . . . will be a sufficient exploratory sample. If the study should prove to be as successful as I hope, I should appeal to one of the foundations for funds to bring the total number of cases to 1000. . . . In the small exploratory study I would secure my case records from students . . . whose families fill this [as outlined above] bill. . . . Thus each student would be in a sense a research assistant and would have to be remunerated for his services."

I have quoted from these letters to show that I had at the time rather grandiose ideas, ideas which, needless to say, have not materialized. One of the interesting things about research is the manner in which projects narrow themselves down in ways not foreseen in advance.

I received the requested grant on May 15, 1931, and at once set to work refining the blank for the family case history which up to that time had been sketched in tentative form only. As actually used, it consisted of 15 mimeographed sheets and the students were instructed to insert extra sheets wherever necessary; so that an average case comprises in the neighborhood of 30 closely written pages. By leaving no spaces between questions and otherwise abbreviating, the whole is reproduced here.

FAMILY ANALYSIS FORM

To be filled out by members of families which have suffered a sudden and apparently lasting decrease in income of at least 25 per cent and in which, up to the advent of the decrease at least, the parents were living together.

1. Give birthplaces of:
   Paternal   Paternal
   Grandfather ....Grandmother ....Father ....
   Maternal   Maternal
   Grandfather ....Grandmother ....Mother ....
2. Years of schooling of Father....of Mother....
3. List places of residence of your father and mother since their marriage with approximate dates for each.
4. Give year of birth and sex of each member of the family residing at home just prior to the decrease in income. Use fictitious names or initials if you prefer.
   Father   Mother   Children:

   Other relatives living with the family: (State relationship)

5. What was the approximate total yearly income of the members of your family residing at home just prior to the decrease?   What is it now?
6. When, as nearly as you can say, did the decrease in income become generally recognized as an existing and probably lasting fact by family members?
7. Discuss briefly whether or not the family has ever really become adjusted to the new situation. Is there at the present writing (state date ......) as much of an equilibrium in the family life as there was before the decrease?

8. Use this sheet and as many more sheets as you need to write one comprehensive paragraph about each of the members of your family listed above. Write of them as they were just prior to the decrease in income and in each instance cover the following points at least:
    1. Physique, health, energy, temperament, mental attitude toward life, and general personality traits such as dull, cautious, sincere, etc.
    2. Principal activities and interests, including occupation, recreation, hobbies, organizations participated in, etc.
    3. Income, if any, and habits with respect to expenditures.
    4. Character of friends and associates.
    5. Attitudes toward other members of the family. (Please be frank about jealousies, antagonisms, etc.)

9. Use this sheet and as many more as you need to discuss the external conditions of your family's existence just prior to the decrease. Touch on the type of neighborhood, the house and yard, the family's material possessions, etc.

10. Use this sheet and as many more as you need to discuss the cultural type of your family just prior to the decrease. Was it strongly influenced by some national heritage such as German, Irish, Jewish? Did the members conceive it as having a certain social role such as an artistocratic family, a middle class family, an intellectual family? Was there any conflict among the family members' conceptions of its cultural type? Of what type was the family in the minds of neighbors?

11. Use this sheet and as many more as you need to discuss the organization of personal relations within the family, just before the decrease. Was there leadership by certain members? or was it domination? Was there rivalry and if so of what kind? Were there cliques within the family? What was the allocation of functions among the members of the family?

12. Use this sheet and as many more as you need to discuss the degree of solidarity in the family just prior to the decrease. Were there common activities in which all participated? Was there family custom and ritual? Were the joys and sorrows of members shared by the whole group? Was there co-operation toward common aims and objectives? Was discipline sympathetic or cruel? Did members have a proud sense of "we" in thinking of the family?

13. Use this sheet and as many more as you need to discuss the opportunities for development within the family possessed by its members just prior to the decrease. Was the development of each a concern of all? Was every effort made to facilitate the pursuance of worthy interests? Were there any evidences of the selfish appropriation of opportunities by some members to the detriment of others?

14. Reread your answer to question (8). Use this sheet and as many more as you need to write paragraphs concerning each member of the family there discussed, telling how the decrease in income has affected the various matters there touched upon.

15–19. Same as question 14 except referring to questions 9–13 respectively.

20. You have discussed the family situation before the decrease in income and after it had its effect. Now use this sheet and as many more as you need to describe what the process of change was. Which elements in the family picture changed first and how did these changes induce the changing of other elements? As a physiologist might trace the complicated, related developments in the physical organism following some one exciting cause, trace the evolutionary steps which your family went through following the decrease in income.

———

It will be noticed that the blank is divided in such a way that the reader can secure a complete picture of the family before the decrease without knowing what happened to it afterward. This was done so that the investigator could come to a conclusion about the original type without being biased by any knowledge of the outcome. Even with this precaution, the problem of unbiased assignment to types became acute, as we shall see, since I had to try several type systems, and, by the time I had gone through the cases three or four times, I knew each one pretty thoroughly and could remember how they eventuated. Under these circumstances the temptation to make the original type such as accorded with the known result and some hypothesis of causation was extremely difficult to resist.

Most of the questions on the blank were purposely made broad and general, rather than narrow and particular. This was to encourage full treatment of every aspect of family life. I felt that I could not designate in advance all the sorts of data which might prove important in constructing family types, so I wished to cast a wide net in the first place. I thought writers might get into the swing of the thing and inadvertently hit upon significant points which would not have occurred to me. I was, and am, aware that other investigators would have taken an opposite course. My belief in this method probably sprang from my training under Professor Cooley. His distrust of a simple question and answer technique was an expression of his profound conviction that social relations are complex in unpredictable ways.

A circumstance which I am the first to acknowledge as a weakness in this set-up was the plan of having these case histories written by only one member of the family with no subsequent independent confirmation. Possibly a very different picture of each family would have been obtained from another source. The only defense possible and the only one I offer is that adequate check-up seemed, and still seems, impossible, for the families obtained came from many parts of the country. The only alternative was to limit the families to ones near enough the University for personal interview. But this would have greatly increased the difficulty of obtaining enough families, and, in addition, many students would not have offered to analyze the home situation if such a check-up had been in prospect.

The form has proven to be most defective in its lack of attention to the decrease itself. Only the amount of it was asked for, though the manner of it came out in all cases. However, it has subsequently been clearly shown that a decrease in income from accustomed sources is only the stimulus to a sociological pressure, not the pressure itself. I should have asked specifically what precise position changes on the symbiotic level accompanied the decrease.

The securing of students able and willing to give the information desired began in the summer of 1931 and, with the exception of the period January–June, 1932, when I was on sabbatical leave, continued until September, 1933. By that time 52 complete records were in my possession, all of them written by students. One trial was made by a person outside of university circles and his inability to give the detailed insight I wanted deterred me from repeating the experiment. Of the 52 cases, two were rejected because they did not conform to the condition that no other crucial event should have occurred since the decrease, a condition the necessity for which was not realized until after I had instructed the first few writers. The method pursued in obtaining cases was simply to announce in sociology classes that the project

was under way and that students would be remunerated for satisfactory analyses. I explained the
project fully to each student, gave him a blank
with the suggestion that he look it through to see
whether he really wished to undertake the work,
and asked him to come back in a few days either
to return the blank if he decided against the proposition, or to clear up questions and receive final in-
structions if he wished to go ahead. When I was
convinced that a student would do a conscientious
job and that he would do his level best to be objective, I let him go ahead without any time limit.
Some finished their first drafts within a week,
others took a month. I read each one carefully as
it was returned, making marginal notations of
questions, omissions or inadequacies and then
called the student back for a conference. When the
shortcomings of his first draft were explained, he
took the blank again and tried to remedy the history's deficiencies. I kept this process up until I
was satisfied, or at least until I seemed to have
reached the individual's capacity for description
and interpretation. Then only did he receive his
remuneration. A few cases were so well done as to
need no revision at all.

In the fall of 1933, having on hand 50 complete
cases which met all the qualifications, I felt it was
time to take stock by trying my hand at analysis.
Since I reported the results of this stock-taking
during the sessions of the American Sociological

Society in December of that year, I shall quote occasionally from that paper.[1]

The first problem was to construct a system of family types. "After canvassing other work in the field, discussing with members of the staff, and experimenting with different conceptual set-ups" on the cases themselves, I determined on a system which used affection, integration of interests and symbiotic interdependence as its three bases. The three degrees of "strong," "mediocre," and "weak" were distinguished with reference to the first, "undifferentiated," "differentiated" and "integrated" with reference to the second, and "strong" and "weak" to the third. "Perhaps the only term which needs explanation is that of integrated interests. By this we mean that the family members so bring their divergent interests back into the family for discussion that all share vicariously the experience of each." Eleven types were constructed by this scheme, as shown in the accompanying table.

"The original plan was to assign each family to a type both before and after the decrease." Mr. Frank Hartung and Mr. Henry Meyer assisted me in attempting this. "Discarding three cases used for tryouts, two of us, working independently, read and assigned type letters to each of the remaining 47. We were disappointed to find that

[1] "The Influence of Severe and Apparently Lasting Decrease in Income upon Family Life," *Publications of the American Sociological Society,* XXVIII, pp. 85–9.

279

FAMILY TYPES

TYPE DEFINITION				SUCCEEDING TRENDS								
				W—MORE SOLIDARITY			X—SAME	Y—TRENDS IRREG.	Z—LESS SOLIDARITY			TOT.
TYPE	AFF.	INTRST.	SYMB. INTDP.	SYMB. ONLY	OTHER WAYS	TOTAL			AFF. WKR.	AFF. NOT WKR.	TOT.	
A		Undif	Str				1					1
B	Str	Integ		3	5	8	2		2	1	3	13
C	Str	Diff			1	1			1		1	2
D	Med	Integ	Str		4	4			1		1	5
E	Med	Integ	Wk		5	5		2				7
F	Med	Diff	Str		5	5		1	1		1	7
G	Med	Diff	Wk	2	7	9		2	1		1	12
H	Wk	Integ	Str									
I	Wk	Integ	Wk									
J	Wk	Diff	Str		1	1						1
K	Wk	Diff	Wk	1	1	2						2
Totals				6	29	35	3	5	6	1	7	50

we had only 44 agreements and 50 disagreements in the 94 type letters assigned. Only 12 of the 47 cases showed agreement both before and after. It became apparent, however, that we agreed in almost every instance on the direction in which the family was moving with respect to each of the three aspects—affection, interests, and symbiotic interdependence. Evidently different interpreters can agree upon the direction of social change much more closely than upon the stage it has reached at any particular time. When we realized this we gave up classifying the situation after the loss of income by the original set of categories and adopted the fourfold classification given in the table. W means more solidarity in at least one aspect and no less in any. X indicates no change, while Y stands for more solidarity in one or more aspects and less in one or more. Z means less solidarity in at least one aspect and no more in any. The two interpreters agreed on these characterizations in all but 3 or 4 cases.

"This procedure did not, however, cure the disagreement as to the proper characterizations for the original family situations. Most of these were easily disposed of through discussion, but in 5 or 6 cases the interpretations of the two readers were so different as to make wholly amicable solutions impossible.

"The factual results shown in the table can be briefly stated. Approximately one-quarter of the cases fell originally in the *B* type, and another quarter in the *G* type. Fourteen per cent were assigned to each of two types, *E* and *F*. The only other clustering was 10 per cent in the *D* type. One may draw rather obvious conclusions from the fact that 87 per cent of the families having strong affection also had integrated interests, while only 35 per cent of those showing affectional difficulties had integrated interests.

"Seventy per cent of these families definitely increased their solidarity following the decrease in income. Nor was this due only to increased consciousness of symbiotic interdependence, as one might perhaps expect. Fifty-eight per cent of the whole number, or 83 per cent of those whose solidarity was increased, improved either in affection or integration of interests or both. The close interdependence of the aspects is shown in the dynamic picture just as it was in the static picture, for only 10 per cent of the cases fell in the *Y* category—that of irregular trends. In 4 of these 5 cases the symbiotic interdependence was that which improved; in one case it was affection. This latter case and the single case in Column 11 are the sole instances of affection remaining the same or getting stronger while solidarity was weakening in some other respect. And when it is pointed out that the *B/Z* case was a quite remarkable family which maintained its emotional ties despite a complete break-up of the home due to the father's commitment to prison, a general trend, to which this is an exception, seems clear. One further generalization may be ventured to the effect that loss of income rarely leaves the family the same. Only 6 per cent of our cases fall in the X group.

"When we come to the main question—to wit, whether we have found definite kinds of families which will make typical adjustments to severe decrease in income—we must answer with a categorical negative. There is no association whatever between the original types and the subsequent adjustments. One could not ask for a more random scattering. This may mean one or more of three things:

1. That a better system of types applied to the material now in hand would yield significant results.

2. That we have not enough accurate material of the right sort to construct such a system of types, and must therefore get more adequate data if we wish to succeed.

3. That this sort of research is either impracticable or unsound.

"I dislike to acquiesce in the last alternative until I have done a great deal more work on these documents. One gets tremendous insight into family life in the well-written cases. It is possible, but not likely, that all we need is a larger number of documents. What seems chiefly required at the moment is better 'hunches' than we have yet had regarding what are the significant aspects of family life for the construction of types that will react characteristically to decrease in income. We can obtain such 'hunches' only by further reading of the cases and the use of imagination, and can evaluate them only by experimentation with type systems."

An important point was not discussed in the paper quoted above because of limitations of space, but it had been investigated; to wit, the question whether the random results were not due to the interference of other significant factors. To test this, I tabulated the size of the community, the original income, the percentage decrease in accustomed income, the number of family members and the lapse of time since the occurrence of the decrease for each case and analyzed whether there were any correlations which would have beclouded relationships between types and ultimate results. My findings were all negative, except in connection with the percentage decrease in income. Here the families which improved averaged a decrease of 59.1 per cent while those which became worse averaged one of 70.3 per cent. There were wide variations in percentage of decrease in each group, however, so that this difference did not seem sufficient to account for the unproductiveness of our results. It did indicate, though, that it was perhaps a mistake to treat the decrease as a similar impinging influence in all cases.

So far my investigation had been a complete

failure. I had been unable to arrive at any generalizations which helped to predict the result when a decrease in income was encountered by a particular family. Obviously these disappointing results, if one could assume that the data were satisfactory, were due either to an unsound system of types or to the hypothesis that the decrease in income was a similar pressure in every case. The more I read the cases over and the more I used my imagination to formulate possible ways out of the impasse, the more certain I became that the latter was at least in part responsible. That the decrease was a factor which, because common, could be ignored in the analysis appeared to be an unwarranted assumption.

The history of my attempts to deal with this problem of the decrease itself as a factor in the situation is an almost perfect example of the muddling, tentative way in which the so-called scientific mind gets ahead. I was certain from the beginning that it was not merely the amount of the decrease that had to be reckoned with, but other facts associated with it. I therefore cast about for a classification of such facts. The first result was the following fivefold scheme:

1. A decrease with no loss of morale by the breadwinner and no change in economic function of the members.
2. A decrease in the chief breadwinner's income with others starting to work.

3. Loss of the chief breadwinner's job with others starting to work.
4. A decrease with no change in economic function but loss of morale on part of breadwinner.
5. A change of chief breadwinner's job.

Casual inspection will show that this classification is of doubtful theoretical validity because it introduces into two classes of impinging influences (Numbers 1 and 4) such an obviously psychological consideration as loss of morale instead of having this appear in the final result. I realized this at the time, but I then saw no likelihood of being able to predict such loss of morale from the original types, and I therefore included it in the decrease situation as a sort of fortuitous circumstance. In conjunction with this classification I developed new ones for the original types and the subsequent situations, but since they did not prove particularly helpful, I will not confuse the reader by detailing them.

When the work of re-classifying all the cases with reference to this set-up was accomplished, it was evident that statistical analysis could not be applied because the cases were scattered into 37 combinations of original type, decrease situation and result. However, it seemed well to work further with these results in other ways. By taking, for instance, all the cases falling into one of the original types and following what happened to them, I began to obtain hints at least at generalizations. For example, it seemed clear that "When there is a decrease with no loss in the breadwinner's morale and no change in function, both a strong family organization and a routine one will stand up." A great many such statements appeared justifiable on the evidence, yet there were situations where cases of the same type went different ways under the same pressure, so that it was clear that the right analysis had not yet been made.

The next trial in the long evolutionary process was in the direction of a simplification of the scheme just discussed. The original types were five, but only three decrease situations were distinguished. The final family adjustments were recorded as an increase, the same, or a decrease under four heads: family pride, mutual helpfulness, affection, and happiness. The three intermediate situations were as follows.

1. A decrease with no loss of morale and no change of function by breadwinner, with or without other members starting to work.
2. A decrease involving loss of morale on part of one of principals.
3. A change in family roles.

In the five original family types we see the first suggestion of the idea of adaptability which ultimately became so central.

1. A family so strong in its organization that it can probably withstand any shock.
2. Fairly well-organized family which can probably withstand (1) above but perhaps not (2) or (3).
3. Families which are well integrated but which have potential weaknesses which may make them unable to cope with any change.
4. Families suffering from cliques or hostilities which can probably weather lesser pressures.
5. Families suffering from cliques or hostilities which can probably not weather any pressure.

Looking back on this set-up, I feel that it was a strange hybrid, an obviously makeshift scheme for analysis. It proved better than any which preceded it, and led the way to the more adequate system later developed. After going through all the cases again and tabulating them according to this scheme, I enlisted the help of Mr. Richard Fuller, instructor in sociology, asking him to do the same thing independently so that we could check the objectivity of my ratings. The chief value of his collaboration, however, was in a quite different direction. He found it difficult to fit the cases into the pre-arranged system of categories and therefore took the opportunity to comment briefly on most of the cases, indicating just why they did not seem to fit exactly. It was after reading over his comments that I began to see light on my problem.

It had been evident for a long time that the inclusion of loss of morale as an accompaniment of a decrease was anomalous. Now Mr. Fuller pointed out that in some cases this had already been foretold by characterizing the family as potentially weak (Type 3 above). Suddenly I saw that loss of morale could and should be a result predictable from the original types, *if these types were based in some way on adaptability as well as on integration.* And I had half-consciously recognized this in the last set of types by the future reference in each description. I was destined to try one more futile system of analysis, however, before I finally found one really workable.

This, the fourth, attempt found me using five types again, with two decrease situations. The types were as follows:

1. High integration, standard of life which makes adjustment to a decrease potentially difficult.
2. Mediocre integration, standard of life which makes adjustment to a decrease potentially difficult.
3. Low integration, standard of life which makes adjustment to a decrease potentially difficult.
4. High integration, standard of life which does not make adjustment potentially difficult.

5. Low integration, standard of life which does not make adjustment potentially difficult.

My decrease situations were now in terms of family roles:

1. Decrease with little change in roles.
2. Decrease with marked change in roles.

I gave up this scheme without even getting to the question of how to classify the ultimate results because there were not fine enough distinctions in either the original types or the decrease situations. Again there were cases classified exactly alike which behaved differently. So I came at last to the general set-up finally employed.

I am ashamed of the fact that I did not see clearly from the start that integration alone would be no basis for predicting the effect of a decrease in income from accustomed sources. It seems now perfectly obvious that if one wished to define types in relation to a change of any kind, flexibility or adaptability with reference to that change was a very important consideration. In the fourth set-up just presented this adaptability was recognized in only a sort of backhand way in terms of the family's standard of life. With more thought I realized that other conditions beside a high standard of living might make a family unadaptable and that, conversely, such a standard need not do so. In the fifth scheme I therefore recognized adaptability as such. Though a change was later made in the analysis of the decrease situations and of the final results, the set of types established at this time proved lasting. These were:

1. Highly integrated, highly adaptable.
2. Highly integrated, moderately adaptable.
3. Highly integrated, unadaptable.
4. Moderately integrated, highly adaptable.
5. Moderately integrated, moderately adaptable.
6. Moderately integrated, unadaptable.
7. Unintegrated, highly adaptable.
8. Unintegrated, moderately adaptable.
9. Unintegrated, unadaptable.

Since the seventh type as here listed did not occur in the sample, we have actually considered only eight types in the body of the study. It was not very difficult to assign families to these types using the criteria for integration and adaptability discussed in Chapter II. In order to be certain that my assignment of cases to types was not a highly subjective and, therefore, unscientific procedure, I called upon Mr. Fuller again, explaining to him what my conception of each type was and asking him to make the classification independently. Furthermore, he was to read only the first half of each analysis so that he would be unprejudiced by the final outcome. (It should be noted that he did this 6 months after his first reading and analysis of the cases so that he recalled how only a very few eventuated.) Of the 50 cases, our assignments coincided in 36. Where he felt it was a close question he recorded a second choice. Of the 14 disagreements, in 7 his second choice was the same as my original one. This left 7 cases of marked disagreement out of 50. Considering the character of the data, we regarded this as reassuring and indicative of considerable objectivity in the classification process. On re-examining the evidence I felt I had made a real error in one case, No. 47, probably because I was biased by my knowledge of its ultimate adjustment. This one I changed from Type VI to Type III. The other six I left as I had them, because it seemed to me they were true borderline cases, and that I could defend my assignments as well as Mr. Fuller could his.

The matter of original types satisfactorily disposed of, I reclassified the conditions associated with the decrease as follows:

1. A decrease with similar roles.
2. A decrease with modified roles.
3. A decrease with changed roles.

This is obviously just a refinement of the last set-up, using three classes of situation instead of two. Though, as will be explained later, the term "role" was unfortunate in this connection, this scheme turned out well and ultimate substitution of "position" for "role" really changed the way the families fell into these classes very little.

I had not, in any of the attempts so far discussed, hit upon a satisfactory way of dealing with the effects of the decrease, nor did I now. In going through the cases again according to the above scheme I merely recorded the family as having "more," "the same," or "less" solidarity, or "conflicting" in this respect. Each case then received a brand of hieroglyphics like this: "HiMa—MR—same," which meant "Highly integrated, moderately adaptable family suffering decrease with modified roles and whose integration remained about the same." When I finished the task of classification this time, there was a gratifying similarity of result in cases of the same type subjected to the same pressure. At last I felt I was on the way to success.

Glancing back over my work sheets, I see that I became obsessed at this point with the idea of quantification. I tried no less than seven different schemes of giving numerical values to the different degrees of original integration and adaptability and to the different pressures associated with the decrease, hoping that by processes of addition and subtraction a numerical result would be reached which would accurately represent the subsequent situation. Although in the majority of instances the best of these schemes worked out fairly well, there were some cases which refused to be quantified in this way. The reason was that I was ignoring the whole notion of vulnerability and critical pressures, concepts which I did not come to until later.

Despite the doubtful success of my efforts at

293

quantification, I was confident of the general feasibility of my last approach and I therefore set about selecting typical cases which could be used to represent different causal sequences in the exposition. I spent much of the summer of 1934 in writing the case narratives which appear throughout the text of this study. It was not until I had almost completed this task that I chanced to read Florian Znaniecki's *The Method of Sociology* and there encountered a set of ideas that furnished a key to some of my difficulties. Let us begin with his notion of closed systems:

"It is the assumption that reality is constituted by innumerable and various *closed systems,* that is, systems each of which is composed of a limited number of elements more intimately interrelated with one another than with any objects which do not belong to the system, and each possessing a specific internal structure which isolates it in certain respects from external influences." [1] Each family in my study was obviously such a system. "Systems . . . change structurally in ways which are not the outcome of their internal forces alone, but are due to disturbing outside influences. No system is totally cut off from outside reality because none of them determines completely and exclusively the nature and relations of all its elements . . . Consequently, the elements of a system do change under the influence of factors which

[1] Florian Znaniecki, *The Method of Sociology,* p. 12.

are not involved in the structure of the system.
. . . There are many cases which show that the
change of one or several elements exercises a disturbing influence on the system as a whole and
may even modify its entire structure.

"Now, such a change in the structure of the
system, since it is not implied in this structure, is
not included in the original knowledge of the system which we have gained by the study of its elements with their connections and expressed in an
exact and rational description. It is something
new and unexpected, something irrational which
must be *explained,* that is, rationalized secondarily.
This is done by conceiving it as the *effect* of some
cause." [1]

As I read this, it seemed to state my problem
more exactly than I had been able to formulate it,
for the whole object of my quest had been to discover the effect of an impinging external influence
upon a number of closed systems, here families.
But so far, Znaniecki was stating explicitly what
I had assumed implicitly. His greatest contribution came where he discussed causal changes in
such systems. Here he demonstrated that the term
"stimulus" has been used in two ways: first, as a
releasing influence for tendencies already active in
the system; and second, as an influence interfering
with tendencies already active. Considering the
first, he says, "Stimulation . . . is not a causal

[1] Florian Znaniecki, *The Method of Sociology.* 16 *passim.*

process at all, for it does not affect either the composition or the structure of the system: the stimulus is such precisely because it brings nothing new into the system; all its influence is derived from the system as it was before. . . . Such events can be dealt with by the original activities of the systems, the problems they raise are either defined in accordance with its tendencies or can be redefined by the latter in a way which makes them soluble, without disturbing the system. . . . It is only the second kind of stimulation which is of importance for the problem of social causality." [1]

This view that systems are potentially capable of coping with some "stimuli" because their occurrence is implied in or soluble by the original system, while incapable of coping with others not so implied or so soluble, was one which I saw to be of tremendous significance for my study. My problem immediately became to discover with what decrease situations each family was potentially able to cope. This led me to the concepts of vulnerability and invulnerability. Instead, then, of judging the final results in terms of better or worse, they were to be judged as a continuation of the original system or an upsetting or reorganization of it.

One more debt I owe to Znaniecki. This is for his term "analytic induction" which he contrasts with "enumerative induction." I had been follow-

[1] Florian Znaniecki, *The Method of Sociology*, pp. 297-8. (Rearranged slightly.)

ing the procedure of analytic induction from the start but had not had a good term for it, nor indeed had I had as clear a concept of what I was doing as I secured from reading his chapter on the subject.[1]

The complementary concepts of vulnerability and invulnerability seemed so apt for my purposes that I went ahead to develop the theory of critical points in the scale of degrees of pressure, on one side of which each type was vulnerable, on the other side of which each was invulnerable. This worked so well for most of the types that for some time I was nonplussed by my inability to apply the concept successfully to the unintegrated types. Reflection, however, brought me to the conclusion accepted in the body of the study, *i.e.,* that these unintegrated families could hardly be regarded as closed systems in the first place, but were rather amorphous entities with very little structure, so that none of Znaniecki's theory was applicable. If this conclusion is a sound one, it only goes to show that one must keep constantly in mind the fundamental assumptions of the concepts with which one is working.

I began writing the original, analytical part of the study as contrasted with the case narratives in the fall of 1934, and I was pretty well through with that process before I struck another snag. For those who are curious about these matters, I

[1] *Ibid.* "Analytic Induction in Sociology," pp. 249-331.

can state quite positively that the stimulation this time came from my class in "Social Process" in which I use Professor Cooley's book of that name. After this class one day it dawned on me as strange that I had made no use of Cooley's concept of the "tentative method" of social process, a concept which was discussed almost daily in this class. I decided to think through my whole problem again from this point of view. Parts of Chapters II and III were inserted as a result. The idea that social forms feel their way by a sort of trial and error process, developing those parts or attributes which seem to "work," and discarding those which do not, was one which obviously should apply to the situation under study. These families were changing as they encountered the depression and some of them were finding difficulty in readjustment. But how was this idea to be fitted to Znaniecki's notion of closed systems? Apparently only the vulnerable families would be thought of as pursuing the tentative process, since by hypothesis the invulnerable ones were unchanged. But this did not seem to be true, since many of the invulnerable families were demonstrably changing in some particulars, such as new members beginning to work. It was then that I became explicitly aware of the need for separating two levels of family life—the symbiotic and the socio-psychological. Here I owe a debt to Professor R. D. McKenzie, for I was familiar with his use of two such levels in his work in human ecology. When this problem presented itself, I immediately defined it in his terms.

With this separation between the symbiotic and the socio-psychological levels once in mind, it was clear that I had been concerned with the latter, and that it was to this level only that the terms vulnerable and invulnerable had reference. This explained how a family might be invulnerable and still illustrate the tentative process, for it could be changing on the symbiotic level. Indeed changes on the symbiotic level were stimuli to the structure on the socio-psychological one, stimuli which were sometimes within the capacities of the socio-psychological structure to deal with them, sometimes not. If not, then the decrease was the critical agent in bringing about disorganization, and perhaps reorganization, on the socio-psychological level.

Once the separation between these two levels was made, it became apparent that the term "role," which in sociological literature has a socio-psychological implication, was improper in describing the conditions involved in the decrease situation and that the term "position" would be preferable. The latter term was therefore substituted for the former throughout the study. This could be done with almost no concomitant revisions in the content because it was symbiotic position rather than socio-psychological role which I had really been talking about all along.

299

The last change in the theoretical aspect of the study was the division of the concept of invulnerability into "firm invulnerability" and "readjustive invulnerability." This came as a result of the realization that in some families which proved invulnerable to the pressure they encountered there was reorganization even on the socio-psychological level. Such reorganization was not explicitly dealt with in Znaniecki's treatment, though his theoretic system is capable of encompassing it. All that is required is the recognition that certain stimuli in certain cases may bring about a gradual shift in the internal arrangements of the closed system without in fact breaking it at any point.

The reader will remember that the sample of 50 was designed to be only exploratory and that, if it yielded results, I planned to try to secure a much larger number for verification and more detailed analysis. This has not been done. The decision not to go ahead was not made explicitly at any one time. Like so many things in life, I drifted into it. The reasons which now support such a decision (or seem to) are: (1) The securing of a large number of family histories of the right sort and written by competent people would be very difficult to arrange even if sufficient financial backing could be obtained; (2) since there were signs of the de pression lifting and since most of the families which have suffered a severe decrease in income suffered it several years ago now, the histories could not be relied upon to be as accurate as those I secured from 1931 to 1933; (3) it is doubtful whether a large sample would yield enough additional knowledge to justify the effort and expense; and (4) perhaps the significance of this study is more in the direction of exemplifying what may be attempted in the way of analytic induction than in the direction of concrete knowledge of family life and processes anyway. At all events I have let the matter rest here for the present.

We are now in a position to view the present study in the larger setting of sociological methodology. This requires that we understand precisely the method employed here, that we compare it with other methods of investigation, and that we attempt to evaluate its worth.

To begin with, it is clear that we have not reached the goal originally set in "A Memorandum Concerning a Proposed Research Technique." We have not tried out the bridging of the gap between case study and the statistical method through coefficients of contingency between combinations of characteristics and resulting adjustments to a particular impinging force.[1] The small number of

---

[1] Others, however, have attacked the same general problem. *See* E. W. Burgess, "Statistics and Case Study," *Sociology and Social Research,* XII, 103–20; R. S. Cavan, P. M. Hauser and S. A. Stauffer, "Note on the Statistical Treatment of Life History Material," *Social Forces,* IX, 200–3; L. L. Thurstone, "Multiple Factor Analysis" *Psychological Review,* XXXVIII, 406–27; and Samuel A. Stauffer and Clark Tibbetts, "Tests of Significance in Applying Westergaard's Method of Expected Cases to Sociological Data," *Journal of the American Statistical Association,* XXXII, 293–302.

families analyzed precludes the use of statistical procedures at all. Instead, we have fallen back on a system of types arrived at by a process of intuitive selection of significant aspects after thorough acquaintance with a series of cases. These types are not of a general nature but are constituted with respect to expected reactions to a particular critical situation, a severe decrease in income. If one were to inquire how these same families would react to a death in the family, no predictions could be made on the basis of these types, particularly because our criteria of adaptability were chosen with reference to a pecuniary crisis.

It is not at all unlikely that, if the original program had been adhered to, a not dissimilar set of types would have emerged, though the probability is that they would have been of a more complicated kind. As intimated in the original memorandum, a statistical technique can draw out of a welter of life situations similar relations and processes which the human mind is unable to disentangle.

Analytic induction of this kind gives us generalizations very like those of the natural scientist. Their truth, however, is much more limited than is the truth of his generalizations. If these are laws at all, they are laws which are true of a particular culture, of modern American life. And as that culture changes, so may these laws be outmoded. That is the penalty which the social scientist must pay for dealing with a universe which has implicit in it what Znaniecki calls the humanistic coefficient.

When we compare this investigation with others which have dealt with similar problems we are made to realize the diversity of method which characterizes sociological research. Since each project adopts its own combination of approach, method, and technique, it would be an endless task to contrast this study with all the other types. However, fundamental points of divergence may be noted.

First, analytic induction has been comparatively rare in sociology. There have been attempts to isolate types of various kinds—types of personality, of communities, of families, even—but these attempts have for the most part not been followed up and built upon. Much more common has been enumerative induction, where the results are in terms of percentages or coefficients of correlation or of contingency. Ogburn's section of *American Marriage and Family Relationships* serves as a fine example. The difficulty in all such research is that the conclusions have to be stated in some such terms as: If factors A, B, C, and D are all present in the original situation of a family which encounters force P, then four times out of five the result will be adjustment X. To say the least, it is tantalizing not to be able to determine why X does not ensue in the fifth case.

Second, many investigators have hesitated to

place as much reliance upon "subjective" data as is done here. They have preferred to rely upon external indices, variations in which can be accurately recorded, instead of upon the memory and interpretation of a "participant observer." The work of Dorothy S. Thomas and her associates is an example in the behavior field, while the development of rating scales for homes is evidence of the same point of view in the field of cultural status. Possibly we could develop some check-list of external factors which would be of significance in studying a problem like the one here investigated, but it would seem more promising to work with attitudes and other "internal" factors.

Attitude research as carried on with various scales and tests is a promising attempt to investigate mental phenomena by objective means. Subjective interpretation is ruled out much more than with documentary material such as we have used. Most attitude investigations have employed the method of enumerative induction, though there is no reason why such research should not lead to the isolation of types. It would have been interesting, certainly, to have paralleled this study with an investigation of the attitudes of the members of the families concerned. Much new insight might have been obtained. Taken alone, however, the attitude study would have had great difficulty in catching the "wholeness" of situations so complicated as those with which we have been concerned.

Third, those who have used types in sociological analysis have not always given them the same empiric basis that we have here. The method of ideal types as exemplified in the work of Max Weber and other German students is one in which the investigator constructs a fictional whole embodying all the characteristics of an entity which are logically necessary and objectively possible. Howard Becker, in discussing the fashioning of such types, says "Beyond doubt the strands we use in our weaving are all spun out of experience, and we certainly intertwine them in harmony with our ideas of what is objectively possible—nevertheless, the resulting fabric is confessedly a heuristic construct, a means of generalization, and is never exemplified, in *all* its precision of pattern, anywhere in the empirical chaos."[1] These ideal types are used as points of reference from which actual entities can be measured, but the latter are not thought of as embodying the type fully, as are the families in this study. The "economic man" is perhaps the most familiar example to Americans of this scientific device.

Undoubtedly the reason for the seeming possibility of setting up types of a more empiric sort in the present study is that we were dealing with situations already greatly simplified by the limitations placed upon the kind of families to be studied

[1] *The Fields and Methods of Sociology* (L. L. Bernard, Ed.), p. 30.

and the kind of change to be encountered by them. Those who have used ideal types, on the other hand, have been analyzing immensely complex situations which were not artificially simplified in this way.

This brief enumeration of other kinds of research gives us perspective for judging the possible contributions from a methodological standpoint of this study. Broadly, it has attempted to use analytic induction upon "subjective" materials to reach empiric types. This is far from a unique undertaking. For example, Mowrer in *The Family* recognized four types of families living in different areas in Chicago,[1] Eubank has classified deserters into types on the basis of social agency documents,[2] and Thomas and Znaniecki devote considerable attention to personality types in *The Polish Peasant in Europe and America*.[3] Perhaps we may say that the methodological significance of this study lies rather in the fact that the types were constructed with a view to the impingement of one kind of new force only. They are types indicating potentialities for specific, not general, adjustment. As such they represent an attempt to break down social reality into simpler, but still unmutilated, parts and processes. Analysis of this general sort could be attempted in many fields and would perhaps supply us with accurate, though minute, gen-

[1] Pp. 188–90. [2] *A Study of Family Desertion*, pp. 37–40.
[3] See the Introduction to Part IV.

eralizations.[1] Their limited scope, however, might not be a defect, for many believe we have been in need of more spade work in restricted areas of theoretical investigation. At least in the past sociology has taken some roads of less promise.

[1] See Znaniecki, *op. cit.*, 319–31 for an excellent discussion of the possibilities of inductive analysis in sociology.

INDEX OF CASES

[1] Cases 33 and 41 are not referred to in the text by number. They are two of the eight cases discussed on pages 61-2.